Praise for **The Office Politics Handbook**

"Having more than 35 years of higher education experi-

is is

suc-

hor

rails

Route # _____

Optional

idly

in a

TO: ___P+S___

nce

our

Code or full name of library

id."

FOR: _____

tate

Code or full name of destination library if different from above

ad-

FROM: **HDS**

ook

ook

that

NOTES/DATE DUE

ips,

my

—Amanda Benson, criminal defense attorney

THE
OFFICE
POLITICS
HANDBOOK

WINNING THE
GAME OF POWER AND
POLITICS AT WORK

JACK GODWIN, PhD

CAREER
PRESS

Pompton Plains, N.J.

THE OFFICE POLITICS HANDBOOK
EDITED AND TYPESET BY KARA KUMPEL
Cover design by Howard Grossman/12E Design
Printed in the U.S.A.

To order this title, please call toll-free 1-800-CAREER-1 (NJ and Canada: 201-848-0310) to order using VISA or MasterCard, or for further information on books from Career Press.

The Career Press, Inc.
220 West Parkway, Unit 12
Pompton Plains, NJ 07444
www.careerpress.com

Library of Congress Cataloging-in-Publication Data

CIP Data Available Upon Request.

For Emilia and Audrey.

Acknowledgments

Thanks to Tracey Culbertson, Lori Harrison, Michelle Loew, Eric Merchant, Mlima Morrison, Caroline Peretti, Josef Preciado, and Janis Silvers, as well as Ben Amata, Ed Baranowski, Bernice Bass de Martinez, Jerry Blake, Judy Boliver, Ric Brown, Karyl Burwell, Kevin Cornwell, Tom Carroll, Emiliano Diaz, Louis Downs, Smile Dube, Virginia Dixon, David Earwicker, Beth Erickson, Buzz Fozouni, Don Gerth, Alex Gonzalez, Alan Haslam, Julian Heather, John Kepley, Tom Krabacher, Kazue Masuyama, Ed Mills, Kathy Mine, Joan Neide, Chevelle Newsome, Melissa Norrbom, Hakan

Ozcelik, Jon Price, Joanne Reilly, Karlos Santos-Coy, Richard Shek, Joe Sheley, Suzanne Swartz, Don Taylor, Catherine Turrill, Ernest Uwazie, Leo Van Cleve, Lori Varlotta, and all my friends and colleagues in the CSU.

Thanks to Dave Bewley-Taylor, Helen Fulton, Branwen Lloyd, Angela Jones, Jon Roper, Ieuan Williams, and everyone at Swansea University.

Thanks to Steffan and Margarita Todorov and everyone in the village of Iskar, Bulgaria.

Thanks to Laura McCaffrey and everyone at the US-UK Fulbright Commission.

Thanks to Anneke Archer, Andrew Hellman, Kira Mills, and everyone at CIES.

Thanks to Amanda Benson and Steve Plesser of Sacramento, California.

Thanks to Jeffery McGraw and Cricket Freeman of the August Agency.

Thanks to Robert S. Cooper, Esq., of Los Angeles, California.

Thanks to Christopher Ruddy and David Alliot of *Newsmax*.

Thanks to Edwin Duerr of San Francisco State University.

Thanks to Richard Chadwick and Shirley Daniel of the University of Hawaii.

Special thanks to Daniel, my brother.

Contents

To Begin With

Interpersonal relationships and politics have fascinated me since I was a child. I grew up in Southern California in the 1960s and '70s, in a fairly traditional American family with a father and mother and three brothers, two older and one younger. I was the middle child: self-sufficient, creative, and slightly introverted. Somewhere along the way, I developed an interest in stamp collecting. Even in those lazy pre-Internet days, stamp dealers had a way of finding stamp collectors, and they sent me parcels full of stamps from all over the world. This necessitated and accelerated my education in geography, history, literature, and, of course, politics.

My hobby, my place in the birth order, and my personality prepared me, somehow, for an apprenticeship in political science. As the middle child, I received less attention, but I had the right temperament and a discreet vantage point from which to observe the political dynamics of daily family life. The first lesson: *Never discuss politics or religion in mixed company*. Politics and religion are notoriously disruptive and so charged with emotion that disagreement and hard feelings are inevitable.[1] This equation—*politics equals emotional tension*—is why talking about politics is strictly forbidden at the dinner table.

What makes politics such a touchy subject? It has to do with power, which is not only a fact of life for everyone, but also a fascinating subject for social scientists. Psychologists may have mixed feelings about the subject but readily acknowledge power is an important dimension in interpersonal relationships.[2] Sociologists may find power hard to define and even harder to operationalize but recognize power as one of many important variables in social interaction.[3] Speaking as a political scientist, I would say power is a fascinating subject and an important dimension in interpersonal relationships and human society. I would also say that power is indeed an essential concept in all the social sciences except one—political science—where power is without a doubt the supreme concept. Power is an objective and inescapable aspect of reality.[4] Power is the basic condition of our existence, and the fundamental problem of our time—our past, present, and future.[5] In political science, there is no ambivalence about power, only fascination. This is what separates the political science from all the other social sciences.

Awhile back, I was talking with one of the students who worked in my office. We were talking about writing. He suggested I read Stephen King's *On Writing*, but I waved him off and told him I was not a fan of King's books. "It's not that kind of book," he said, "it's a memoir about writing. It came out in 2000, after the car accident. You should read it." So I did.

I remember one passage in particular: Writers are also readers, King said, and fans of other writers. Often when you read something so good, you say to yourself, *I could never write that well.* That is, until the moment when you read something so bad you say to yourself, *I can do better than that.*[6] I can remember the book I was reading when I had King's Epiphany. I can even remember the offending clause: "By the beginning of the last decade of the twentieth century..." wrote the very famous writer, who shall remain anonymous. I did the math and decided "By 1990" would have been more economical. King's advice planted the seed that grew into my first book, then another, and now this one.

It has been said you need to learn a language to study a language.[7] What's the difference between this fine example of tautology and King's assertion that writers must also be readers and fans of other writers? You must be a *fan* of the language. Being a fan is different from being a student in one important respect: Enthusiasm is given. Fans don't need to be goaded into doing homework. To be a fan of the language means you will (enthusiastically) devote hours, weeks, and years to acquire the necessary knowledge and skills by studying, practicing, reading, writing—and rewriting. I would say being a fan of politics requires equal devotion and enthusiasm. Unfortunately, enthusiasm is not enough because politics is deeply rooted in human nature.

The specific idea for this book goes back to my days as a graduate student at the University of Hawaii. There was a question on my comprehensive exam (the test doctoral candidates need to pass before they officially begin writing the dissertation) about the role of power in political science, a subject that has interested me for as long as I can remember. Well, I passed the exam and went on to graduate, but I continued to think about the question.

A few years later, I was in San Francisco doing a radio interview on *The Ronn Owens Program*. At the end of the hour-long interview, the topic turned to the crowded field for California's upcoming gubernatorial election. Given the sorry state of affairs in California, asked a grimacing Ronn, *Why oh why* would anyone want that job in the first place? Politics is about power, I said, and certain individuals minimize other things they value in their lives, such as wealth, health, respect, morality, or love for the attainment of power. These individuals resort to power-seeking when they calculate political behavior will serve their interests more than other types of behavior. Their expectation is that power will compensate for the subordination (or deprivation) of other values, which is how these individuals justify their power-seeking behavior. If and when these individuals have values other than power, it is because those values help feed their appetite for power.

In short, some people thrive on power, but we are all political animals.

Aristotle coined this phrase a long time ago. Being called an animal is not necessarily an insult, but not quite a compliment either. What justifies this summary judgment? Political behavior is an essential element of human nature, a primitive and instinctive element. In this context, the word *primitive* is not judgmental but mindful that politics is perfectly natural and that people have been engaged in unarmed political conflict since the beginning of time. "Politics" is not a foreign entity that has invaded the species the way bacteria infects your body and makes you sick. Political behavior is hardwired into the human race.

Nonetheless, some people feel squeamish about politics and power the way others cannot stand the sight of blood. People who suffer from hemophobia find blood repulsive—any kind of blood from humans or animals, and even pictures of blood. The origin of this fear is unknown. Similarly, what causes fear of politics or fear of power? I cannot say for sure, but I think the origin is buried deep in human nature, in the primitive, instinctive collective element shared by the entire human species. I believe this to be true even though people obviously have the ability to perceive right and wrong, and can demonstrate great capacity for love. Politics can bring out the best in people, but do not let this mislead you—politics is about power.

What is power? Power is anything that facilitates control by one human over another. Power is the concept that distinguishes political science from all other social sciences. Without this concept, there would be no need for political science at all. What is politics? Politics is any social situation in which power is introduced. The essence of politics is self-interest, which is the most reliable standard to measure the success of political action. Other fields have their own standards, their own ways of measuring success, but nothing supersedes the autonomy of the political sphere.

However, *The Office Politics Handbook* does not belong to the genre of horror fiction. *It's not that kind of book.* There is nothing supernatural about it, but that should not prevent us from picking up a few tips from Stephen King's memoir on the craft of writing. In particular, he uses the toolbox as a metaphor to describe all the skills, devices, and *elements of style* a writer needs to get the job done. This metaphor is helpful for our purposes because it enlarges the vocabulary of politics beyond images of warfare and weapons. In addition, the toolbox metaphor highlights the idea that politics and writing are skills you can cultivate. The more you cultivate them the sharper they become, not merely in terms of *how-to*, but also *how-much-to*.

This idea of *how-much-to* (what I call political economy) is important because politics is about power, the acquisition of power, the distribution of power, and the uses and abuses of power. Politics can be horrifying, insulting, and cruel, but not necessarily violent. This is where the idea of *how-much-to* enters into the equation. Power is a useful instrument, but a blunt instrument for those who habitually rely on threats of punishment or promises of reward to force someone's submission. The key to politics is to use only as much power as required, which is why you need to know about different types of power, how to use them, and, equally important, how to recognize them when someone else is using them against you.

Knowing about, recognizing, and using different types of power is an essential step toward developing your capacity for leadership. Leadership is one instrument in the political toolbox, and the one I hope you learn to reach for first. This is why I wrote this book. And this is why you must have a full toolbox. Leadership does not rely on threats of punishment or promises of reward to force submission. Leadership does not emanate from your place on the organizational chart, but from the *follower's* response. Leadership requires finesse. Leadership requires consent. Leadership is what separates you from the average political animal.

In this book you will find seven chapters:

Chapter 1: The Political Animal explains why people are political animals, and why they engage in power-seeking behavior.

Chapter 2: First Principles summarizes the peculiar logic and laws of politics, which are rooted in human nature and impervious to our preferences. This chapter also explains how your personal characteristics affect the way you learn, the way you communicate, how you send and receive signals, and how you classify information.

Chapter 3: The Political Mystique discusses why "the personal is political" and vice versa. This chapter also describes the structure of political conflict, different instruments of power, and the process of pattern recognition.

Chapter 4: The Inward Journey helps the reader understand the cultural and collective forces at work in human nature, and the occasionally aggressive characteristics of the political animal. This chapter also explains the meaning of self-mastery.

Chapter 5: Introduction to Archetypes introduces the universal forms and patterns of behavior known as archetypes. This chapter shows you how to use political archetypes to acquire influence over important decisions; to disrupt your adversaries' plans, exploit their weaknesses, and win without fighting.

Chapter 6: The Gods of Micropolitics is the core of the book and describes the eight political archetypes: the Servant-Leader, the Rebel, the Mentor, the Recluse, the Judo Master, the Resister, the Opportunist, and the Survivor.

Chapter 7: What's it All About? summarizes the book, delves into my personal journey, and explains why superior force is no match for intelligent strategy.

A Note on the Pronoun

I cannot remember how many books I have read in which the author used the masculine pronoun for the sake of convenience. Although the target audience of this book is not gender specific, I have chosen to do the opposite. My professional life is full of hardworking, smart, and educated women. My home life is too. ("Hardworking, smart, and educated" ranks high in my value system.) My wife and I are raising a daughter together. I hope she reads this book someday, so with her in mind I am using the feminine pronoun whenever possible.[8]

Part I

Defining the Art

Chapter 1

The Political Animal

Every part, brain and body, nerve tissue and fiber, was keyed to the most exquisite pitch; and between all the parts there was a perfect equilibrium or adjustment. To sights and sounds and events which required action, he responded with lightninglike rapidity.

He perceived and determined and responded in the same instant. In point of fact the three actions of perceiving, determining, and responding were sequential; but so infinitesimal were the intervals of time between them that they appeared simultaneous.

Life streamed through him in splendid flood, glad and rampant, until it seemed that it would burst him asunder in sheer ecstasy and pour forth generously over the world.

—Jack London, *Call of the Wild* (1903)

This book is for people who dislike power games, but who also recognize that politics takes place wherever there are people: between supervisors and employees, teachers and students, parents and children, and among friends, partners, and spouses. Politics takes place in every country and every culture. It takes place in formal and informal situations and in all kinds of organizations: governments, corporations, academic and religious institutions, and households.

Fortunately, there is no monopoly on power in our modern society, but a diverse "power market" of sorts (imperfect and inefficient and irrational though it is) where individuals and institutions compete with one another for a share of power. If you would like to have more power in your life and greater participation in decision-making on a human scale—with your boss, coworkers, friends, or family members—then keep reading because this book will help shift the balance of power in your favor. If you were asking yourself why you bought this book, now you know. After all, who among us has not been party to an altercation that ended badly, and then replayed the scene in our heads thinking what we could have said and done differently?

There is a mystique to politics, which gives special significance to power, the acquisition of power, and the distribution of power.[1] This mystique goes down to the very foundations of human life and satisfies our most basic instincts for power, freedom, and security. Generations may come and go. Entire nations may emerge and disintegrate in a few decades. Political leaders may take control and reign supreme, for a while, until opposing forces and competing influences push the status quo out of equilibrium again. Naturally, new leaders come to power. Naturally, opposition factions resist and the cycle begins again. Thus, power is distributed and redistributed in accordance with the laws of politics.

Other scholars may disagree, but through it all I see no evidence that human nature has changed (meaning improved or moved forward). I say this despite countless cultural developments, discoveries, inventions, and technologies unknown to our ancestors, and hundreds of years of so-called progress.[2] These novelties always seem more important in the moment, the same way events in close proximity seem more important than events far away. Although this tendency certainly leaves the impression that recent events are more important than historic events, I believe our long journey out of the cave has had little or no effect on our human nature. This is not because human nature is dead or dormant, but because it is complete. When I say complete, I do not mean perfect. Human nature is primitive, instinctive, occasionally decent, and often repulsive. However, this idea of completion calls for objectivity and realism on our part if we are to understand human nature, not just the average but the outer limits, the dark side and the brightness. We all have our share of human nature, and therefore, we all have the potential and capacity for politics. To dispute this is to disregard the conditions of your own nature. No one—no man or woman—can escape this essential constraint.

Within this constraint, however, there is still room to maneuver. This gap may be smaller than the head of a pin and the interval may last no more than a second, but it is manageable. This is where you should concentrate your attention and energy, not denying your humanity but getting acquainted with it and taking account of your political instincts. Disregarding these conditions—the potential and capacity for politics—will not protect you. You must recognize your human nature so you can recognize it in others. This is critical in life and in the office for dealing with friends and adversaries alike, for minimizing politics in relationships and defending yourself when necessary.

Where do we begin? First, I should say this book is a declaration of independence as well as a doctrine of *interdependence*. Why? Politics is interactive and responsive, and thus requires you to get up close with your adversary. There is a difference between theory and practice, a difference between reading about politics and physically experiencing the results of your actions. It takes a special skill to stay objective when you are in the thick of it, even when events you initiated are unfolding just as you hoped and expected. Fortunately, this is a skill you can cultivate.

To ensure objectivity and realism on our part, our understanding of politics must begin with the individual, but we cannot leave it there. Any understanding of politics based entirely on the individual would be incomplete. Therefore, we must venture inward, toward your personal psychology, outward into the space between us all, and downward toward the basic elements of human nature. Politics is an interpersonal situation, which by definition requires at least two people interacting, taking cues from and responding to one another in an ongoing spiral of give and take.[3]

Activities such as eating or sleeping, for example, are natural but not necessarily social. Sexuality may or may not be as strong an instinct as politics, but politics is similarly always a social behavior requiring at least two participants. Political animals are power-seekers whose success depends on convincing or neutralizing those who are resistant or indifferent. If there are power-seekers who minimize other goals in their lives for the sake of power, there are also power-yielders who relinquish power because they put a premium on other values.

The Space Between Us All

Disneyland was about an hour away from where I grew up in Southern California and my family visited the park every year or so. One of my favorite rides was Monsanto's *Adventure thru Inner Space*. It was located in an area of the park called "Tomorrowland," which in those days showcased an idealized (and corporatized) vision of the future. *Adventure thru Inner Space* opened in the late 1960s but eventually closed to make way for a new *Star Wars* ride. While it was open, it was more than a ride: It was truly an adventure.

Inner space—as opposed to outer space—was the subatomic world. The idea of *Adventure thru Inner Space* was to shrink you down so you could actually see the world at the subatomic level. You began by entering a giant microscope, which was a little frightening because you could see the riders in front of you—now miniaturized—exiting the microscope. You kept shrinking, first smaller than snowflakes, then smaller than the crystals of a snowflake until you were small enough to pass through the snowflake's walls and actually see water molecules. You kept shrinking and shrinking until you could fit inside an atom. Time practically stood still as elementary particles bounced off one another in slow motion. After that, you began growing back to normal size until you reemerged from your *Adventure thru Inner Space* into the bright sunlight.

If we could take an adventure through political inner space, could we see the fundamental structure of politics from the inside? What if we stripped away all the dynasties and conquests, all the governments, political parties, and factions, and reduced politics down to the essentials? Would we see people bumping into one another the way protons and neutrons collide? Surely this would not be random. Surely, there is order at some level even if it all appears random to the untrained eye. Think about nuclear energy for a moment. In nuclear fission, the nucleus breaks apart and releases a tremendous amount of energy. In nuclear fusion, smaller particles combine to form a larger nucleus, which also releases a tremendous amount of energy. This is politics at the elementary level: the interpersonal level. The more closely we study politics at this level, the more we will discover what powerful forces come from the smallest sources.

All politics is local. You have probably heard this quotation, which is attributed to Tip O'Neill, former speaker of the House of Representatives during Ronald Reagan's White House years.[4] The term is synonymous with retail politics, which means campaigning door to door and canvassing potential voters one at a time. In common usage, "retail" means selling goods and services to individual consumers. The consumer is the end-user and has no intention of reselling to anyone else. Retail politics also has a pejorative connotation—buying votes—but this is not what I mean. I am referring to the personal interaction between power-seekers and power-yielders. This interaction is an exchange analogous to microeconomics, except it deals with individual *political* units instead of individual *economic* units.

If you position yourself at this level, you get an idea of where micropolitics takes place. For the student and practitioner of micropolitics, this is the Archimedean Point—where you would stand if you wanted perfect objectivity uncorrupted by cultural or emotional influences. (It was Greek mathematician Archimedes who claimed he could move the Earth if only he had a big enough lever and a place to stand.) The Archimedean Point is imaginary and unattainable, which makes it the ideal metaphor for the workbench of micropolitics.[5]

Now, standing at this workbench, please focus your attention on *the space between us all.* This space is any kind of formal or informal social situation, wherever there are people who are interdependent and where the distribution of power is asymmetrical. In the workplace, the best example of this would be the formal meeting, with everyone gathered around a big conference table. Everyone knows these meetings are a waste of time. However, if you apply a *political* standard instead of, let's say, a *productivity* standard, the conference room is transformed into a political space and the meeting into an arena where people compete for power and prestige.

When you consider micropolitics, you would be well advised to set aside your spatial presumptions because the physical geography of micropolitics is very small—sometimes the width of a conference table, sometimes no more than the space between two dancers. Micropolitics is dynamic, interactive, responsive, and intimate. This is where you should look because this is where micropolitics comes to life.

When you know *where* micropolitics takes place, you know where to build your workbench, and where to set your toolbox while you read and play the field. This is the term—the field— that French sociologist Pierre Bourdieu used to describe the space where social interaction takes place. For Bourdieu, the field was a social space with its own structure, its own rules, and its own autonomy.[6] However, the social space Bourdieu wrote about isn't all that interesting to me (speaking as a political scientist) until the moment power is introduced, because that's the moment the social space becomes political. As I said at the beginning, politics is any social situation in which power is introduced. Power is the concept that makes political science distinct from sociology, psychology, and all other social sciences.

A long time ago, I had a professor in college who said there were only two things in life worth doing. One was making love. The other was making distinctions. This well-rehearsed line always drew an enthusiastic response from a lecture hall full of undergraduate students. When I speak of power, I am not just talking about controlling other people in your organization. I am also referring to your autonomy, your liberty, and of course your self-mastery. This is the distinction. Your autonomy feeds your soul in time of trouble. It gives you a sense of detachment and a new perspective, an Archimedean point of view, which insulates you from cultural or emotional influences. And it gives you leverage; not the kind that lets you move the world but the kind that lets you see the world. It gives you the priceless gift of insight. You can use this insight to make distinctions. Most people see the difference between good and evil. Fewer can make subtler distinctions, such as those pertaining to the laws of micropolitics, which we will discuss in Chapter 2.

It may seem trivial, but making distinctions is what lets you be *in* the world but not *of* the world, and gives you the kind of detachment you see in a forensic pathologist or medical examiner (ME). In those popular crime-scene-investigator shows on television, invariably there is a scene in the ME's lab with a corpse lying on the examination table. The ME lists the contents of the deceased's stomach: partially digested pepperoni pizza, cherry Coke, and cheesecake. It would be nice if micropolitics worked this way; it would be most advantageous to have the ME's cool scientific detachment. Unfortunately, your political adversaries will not lay down long enough for you to do a post-mortem, which means you have to read the field, list the alternative courses of action, consider the consequences of *inaction*, and then make your move all in the span of a few moments. (This requires good timing and self-mastery, which we will cover in Chapter 4.) How do you recognize your adversaries at work? They could be anyone. Throw out the organization chart and ask yourself, *Who exercises veto power over my decisions? Who opposes or obstructs me, directly or indirectly? Who competes with me for resources or recognition?* You may not like the answers, but you must ask nonetheless.

Politics Is Serious Play

Why do we so often associate politics with game-playing? In *The 48 Laws of Power*, American author Robert Greene claims repeatedly that power is a game. You may find the urge to play inter-office political games irresistible and you may consider yourself the ultimate realist because of your skillful manipulation of people in your organization. However, I think most people who play political games lack self-discipline and have no idea of the consequences of their actions. They may succeed in hurting or humiliating their adversaries but are almost certainly hurting themselves in the process. In any case, please don't waste your time with this kind of game-playing.

Richard Chadwick, my mentor at the University of Hawaii, had an idea he called The Deficit Theory of Education. Here is Chadwick's no-nonsense explanation: "Psychologists have weak egos, mathematicians can't add, anthropologists don't understand culture, sociologists are generally from 'out groups,' political scientists have power hang-ups, and so on. The deficit is something they value and see themselves as having less of than they want or need. Fear of not overcoming that deficit is their motivation."[7] The main difference between those who make a lasting contribution to their chosen field (eliminating the deficit) and those who do not, is that contributors transform their motivation into play, then transform their play into serious purpose, while those who cannot or will not transform their motivation search for some form of revenge on the world. (Batman's nemesis, the Joker, for example, or Superman's nemesis, Lex Luthor.)

The difference has to do with the distinction between ordinary play and serious play. Ordinary play may require imagination and creativity; it may help you learn important social skills and society's informal rules and expectations. All of this is invaluable. But serious play serves a purpose. Serious play requires persistence toward a goal. The distinction between ordinary versus serious play is analogous to the distinction between seduction and courtship: To seduce is to mislead; to court is to woo. When you court someone, you are trying to earn their love, not fool them. If you took a snapshot of seduction and courtship, the difference would be indistinguishable. This is because the difference between seduction and courtship is persistence, which no snapshot could capture in a moment of time. Courtship is serious play.

How is this relevant? If there is a deficit in your personality—something you value *and* see yourself as having less than you want or need—it may create an irrational fear that makes you potentially harmful to yourself or others. As stated, politics is always a social situation—and an interactive situation—and much depends on the power, prestige, and respect that people confer on you. Your self-image is mostly a reflection of the image others have formed of you, and your self-esteem is greatly dependent on your status in the groups you value.[8] For most people, having the love and respect of friends, family, and coworkers is sufficient. You don't need to run for high office. However, the need for prestige or status is rooted in human nature, which means it is rooted in your nature.

Micropolitics serves a purpose, and thus requires persistence. The purpose is to teach people who are less powerful to defend themselves against people who are more powerful; to break your adversary's hold on you rather than merely responding to one attack after another; and to develop your ability to defend yourself rather than your first-strike/counter-strike capabilities. I am certainly not suggesting you should make a habit of "punching above your weight." (This expression comes from boxing and describes a fighter who punches like a fighter in a heavier weight class.) On one level, punching above your weight means exceeding expectations, which is an admirable characteristic. On another level, it means you are out of your league. It is permitted and sometimes required to venture out of your league—to punch above your weight—in matters of self-defense. But this is very different from causing trouble or provoking conflict. Consequently, as an organizing principle, think of micropolitics as a firewall that allows you to go out to meet trouble but does not invite it or provoke it.

The key to micropolitics is self-mastery. Like many important ideas, self-mastery is multidimensional. One element is self-control, which legendary author and management consultant Stephen Covey described as the ability to subordinate an impulse.[9] This personal element of self-mastery is indispensable but neglects the social element of self-mastery. The distinction is between personal power (the power *to* or the power *of*) and social power (the power over someone).[10] As stated, politics is a social affair, and any understanding of micropolitics based entirely on the individual would be incomplete. For the same reason, achievement of self-mastery requires both halves (the personal and the social) as well as a feedback loop, to be complete.

Some questions to be answered: How do you interpret political behavior in your office? How do you perceive political behavior and categorize political events? Politics can be crude and undisciplined, but it does not have to be. Power games are of limited strategic value and work best at the tactical level no matter how creative they may be. When people blame "politics," they are really announcing their own limited understanding. My objection to most books on office politics is the way they trivialize the subject, as though playing power games were some sort of harmless entertainment. My other gripe is with the way most management consultants lump together everything they dislike and then dismiss it all as "politics."

One notable exception to this is Peter Block's *The Empowered Manager*. This is an excellent book, which teaches managers how to assert themselves, take personal responsibility to be better leaders and stewards, and transform the bureaucracy into an organization you can believe in.[11] Unfortunately, Block's thesis is that politics is inherently negative, destructive, and manipulative, and that the antidote to politics is empowerment, meaning "positive" political skills. If you think all politics is bad and we would all be better off if there were less of it, this may indicate an underdeveloped sense of politics.

What if, instead of blaming politics, you came to the realization that many of your problems are the result of the loss of political instinct and the lack of political imagination? Is it possible for mere mortals to master micropolitics simply by reading a book? Is *The Office Politics Handbook* just like any other book that promises to change your life? You buy the book and it makes you feel assertive, for a while. You read a few pages and it makes you feel euphoric, for a while. Then you fall back to earth and feel worse than ever. Is the self-improvement bubble like any other economic bubble—dot-com, stock, real estate—in which expectations rise to an unsustainable level only to burst and crash later on?

As we proceed through the chapters ahead, let us enlarge the meaning of self-improvement beyond chicken soup. Let us agree to make political triage a top priority. In an emergency room or on a battlefield, you must ration care because demand so clearly exceeds supply. Your duty is to treat the sickest people and to treat as many people as possible, but you must still take care of yourself. In order to succeed at this, you must remember you are surrounded by politics and you are under attack. Time is limited. Planning is inadequate. Resources are scarce and everything comes with an expiration date. You are a political animal, which means you can learn to separate physical pain from emotional pain, particularly the kind you suffer from indignation and insult. As your political mastery increases, so will your ability to help the people around you: your superiors, subordinates, and peers.

Of course, if you don't work in an emergency room or on a battlefield, you may not share my sense of urgency. But don't let this deceive you. Don't let the Myth of Helplessness exempt you from standing up for yourself. This myth is based on two false assumptions. First is the assumption that there is no difference between what you cannot do and what you refuse to do. You may be the victim of bullying at work, for example, or you may see bullying but refuse to say or do anything because you feel helpless. Second is the assumption of the "head honcho," and it goes something like this: "I'm helpless because my present position is weak, but things will change when I'm head honcho." This is how weak people—because of their place on the organizational chart—rationalize *not* taking responsibility. This is also how ambitious people fool themselves because they underestimate how "completely sucked up by the system" they will be by the time they climb to the top of the ladder.[12] Rejecting the Myth of Helplessness will clarify a few things for you (particularly when it comes to your abilities and your responsibilities) and is thus a requisite step toward self-mastery.

Although I am a political scientist by training, I am not trying to formulate a comprehensive theory, but to present what I have learned based on my personal experience and my academic training. My mentor at Hawaii, Richard Chadwick, said something else I will always remember: "A PhD is nothing but a learner's permit." This means I am still an apprentice and this book is a working hypothesis. *Working* is the operative word because it abides by the Japanese art of finding beauty in things that are impermanent, imperfect, and incomplete.[13]

This puts the field of micropolitics in the category of creative science, meaning we cannot—we must not—limit ourselves to conventional dogma on the subject.[14] As stated, my goal is to teach political self-defense, to teach people who are less powerful how to defend themselves against people who are more powerful. Your goal—if you will—is to bring micropolitics to life. Your goal, if you are willing to admit you cannot solve this problem on your own, is to grow beyond yourself, become someone different. If you want to become someone different, we must go on a journey together. Before you turn the page, remember there is *a small universe of possibility* in the space between us all. There is the possibility for self-improvement for sure, but there is also the possibility for authentic leadership, not the kind that comes from the corner office, but that comes from your moral authority.

Chapter 2

First Principles

When you show that odd flash of contextual intelligence, I forget your generation can't read, Clarice. The Emperor [Marcus Aurelius] counsels simplicity. First principles. Of each particular thing, ask: What is it in itself, in its own constitution? What is its causal nature?

—Hannibal Lecter to Clarice Starling in *Silence of the Lambs*

In the beginning, God created heaven and earth. On the fifth day, God created a man named Adam and let him rule the earth. Then God created a companion for Adam, a woman named Eve. Eve gave birth to sons Cain and Abel. Cain was a farmer and Abel was a shepherd. Abel offered the fruits of his labor to God, which pleased God but made Cain jealous and angry. Cain lured his brother Abel into a field, where he killed him. This original act of violence, found both in the Bible (Genesis 4:1–8) and the Qur'an (Surah 5 Al Ma'idah: 27–30) highlights an essential principle of micropolitics: *The laws of politics are rooted in human nature.*[1]

This essential principle has endured thousands of years because it permits the most objective and least sentimental understanding of politics. In the mid-20th century, German-American scholar Hans Morgenthau wrote a classic textbook called *Politics among Nations*. Morgenthau's book is useful because his theory of international politics is rooted in human nature, as is our theory of micropolitics. Now, I realize the scope of our inquiry is smaller, but if Morgenthau's theory is truly rooted in human nature, and if it is as objective and as unsentimental as he claims, then his theory should apply equally to micropolitics. Let us see if it is possible to adapt Morgenthau's principles of political realism and squeeze them into the space between us all.[2]

1. According to political realism, the laws of politics are rooted in human nature. These laws are objective and impervious to our preferences. If you want to improve society or your organization or your own political situation, you must first understand the laws of politics. If you try to change them, you will fail. If you ignore them, you may get lucky for a while, but eventually your luck will run out. The laws of politics give meaning to the facts in a specific situation. These laws suggest alternate courses of political action and also show how to evaluate the results of political action. These laws, rooted as they are in human nature, have not changed in thousands of years, since the ancient philosophers of China, India, and Greece first attempted to discover and articulate them.

2. The main concept of political realism is that politics is about power. Understanding this concept is essential to reading the field and understanding the facts in any given situation. This concept is what distinguishes political science from all other social sciences.[3] Without the concept that politics is about power—the acquisition of power, the distribution of power, the uses and abuses of power—there would be no difference between political and non-political action. There would be no micropolitics, no international politics, and no need for political science at all. Whereas we can assume that politicians, elected officials, and other office-holders think and act in terms of politics, we cannot make this assumption about everyone else. However, we can ascertain the political acumen of our coworkers by carefully reading the field and identifying the alternative courses of action someone would take if she was acting in terms of politics. Regardless of one's motives, regardless of whether one's goal is to make the world a better place, it is always possible for the plan to backfire. You can end up making things worse or you can end up with results you did not want or even predict. Political realism imposes discipline and brings order to your thinking, but this has nothing to do with good intentions. Good Intentions do not guarantee political success. Politics has its own peculiar logic, which does not require good intentions. However, it does require you to distinguish between *what is possible* under certain circumstances and *what would be desirable* in general.

3. Power is anything that facilitates the control of one human over another, and politics is any social relationship that serves this end.[4] Although politics is about power, the meaning of power may change depending on time and place because people have different interests at different times. Interest is the essence of politics because interest is the most reliable standard by which we can judge political action. In politics, interest is synonymous with special interest, meaning a relationship exists between an individual or group and a specific privilege or financial benefit.

In management, we call people "stakeholders" when they have a stake, an investment, or an interest in a project or organization, and can influence *or be influenced by* the project or organization's activities. In politics, interests and special interest groups—the stakes and the stakeholders—are inseparable. No matter how virtuous people may be in public, very few people are capable of making long-term sacrifices contrary to their interests. This kind of behavior is simply inconsistent with human nature. This does not mean there are no examples of long-term sacrifice in human history, but it means you should not build your foundation on this false assumption. Because the laws of politics are impervious to our preferences, it is impossible to change the world either by confronting or ignoring these laws. Before you take political action, and before you define your specific interest in any situation, you should take this into account.

4. Micropolitics recognizes the possible (perhaps inevitable) contradiction between morality and successful political action. At the interpersonal level, this is not something we can afford to ignore or even underestimate. However, because we understand politics within the context of human nature, we can filter politics (what we *can* do) and morality (what we *should* do) through the peculiar logic of politics. That is, we must always consider the ethical implications of political action. Of course, you can rationalize your behavior after the fact, but it would be wiser to consider the ethical implications before you act. Different political actions have different ethical implications, which you should take into account while you consider alternative courses of action. This transforms morality from a universal abstraction into a hard choice between what is possible and what would be desirable.

5. In politics, you must learn to separate political action from morality. This does not necessarily mean politics is immoral, but neither does it mean God is on your side. You must behave

ethically, but do not confuse your will with God's will. You cannot measure your success in terms of morality because power is so corrosive it distorts your judgment. Power plays tricks on your mind and convinces you of your own moral superiority. How much resistance do you think you can offer to counteract the corrosive and uncontrollable effects of power? As stated, interest is the essence of politics and the most reliable standard by which we can judge political action. This applies equally to the actions you take and the actions others take. This is where a deep understanding of human nature—where the laws of politics are rooted—can make reality intelligible and serve as a substitute for experience. In this sense, mastering micropolitics is better than experience if it saves you from corruption and embarrassment.

6. Some people want to abolish politics—as if this were possible. Others want to devalue it, and rank it lower than forms of human behavior.[5] Both approaches are counterproductive. Politics is equal to any other field of human endeavor. As a student and practitioner of politics, it is possible to acknowledge the existence of other fields without subordinating politics to any of them. Other social sciences have their place, their own standards, their own ways of measuring success, but none can supersede the "autonomy of the political sphere." This does not diminish other fields because each has a proper sphere and function. Just as we distinguish between different facets of human nature, however, we can and must distinguish between politics and these other fields. We must designate a unique sphere for politics and apply standards of thought according to its own peculiar logic. As stated, the laws of politics are objective and impervious to our preferences, which inevitably provokes resistance, a kind of learning disability that other fields, such as anthropology, economics, sociology, and psychology, do not face.

Before we move on, we should compare Morgenthau's definition of power with other interesting commentary (from other disciplines) on the subject. Harold Lasswell defined power as the threat of deprivation of something of value.[6] Max Weber defined power as "the probability that one actor within a social relationship will be in position to carry out his own will despite resistance, regardless of the basis on which this probability rests."[7] Presidential biographer James Burns defined power as a "*relationship* in which two or more persons tap motivational bases in one another and bring varying resources to bear in the process."[8] According to Austrian-American diplomat and author Robert Strausz-Hupé, "Power is a dynamic relationship between men who in their conscious actions take their cue from where they think power lies and what it will be used for."[9] We will explore this idea of social and interpersonal cues later on. Meanwhile, credit for the shortest definition belongs to Strausz-Hupé: "politics is the pursuit of power."[10]

Psychologist Erich Fromm had this interesting observation on the power relationship: "The common element in both submission and domination is the symbiotic nature of relatedness. Both persons involved have lost their integrity and freedom; they live on each other and from each other, satisfying their craving for closeness, yet suffering from the lack of inner strength and self-reliance which would require freedom and independence, and furthermore constantly threatened by the conscious or unconscious hostility which is bound to arise from the symbiotic relationship."[11] Applying Fromm's standard—a psychological standard—political behavior (or power-seeking) is a psychological disorder based on submission and domination. Neither party has integrity, freedom, or independence. Both parties are hostile and both lack inner strength and self-reliance.

Another author wrote a book-length essay comparing power to pornography. People are *aggressive* and irrational, he said, and society is *repressive* and irrational. Political repression, like sexual repression, inevitably leads people to search for substitute forms of gratification. When political behavior becomes a substitute form of gratification, it becomes corrosive and abusive.[12] Yet another author theorized that the potential for sadism (deriving pleasure from someone else's pain, suffering, and humiliation) is rooted in human nature, as is the potential for masochism (deriving pleasure from your own pain and suffering), and the only reason people engage in political behavior is because they're frightened and lonely, and they seek to relieve their isolation by seeking to control, or to be controlled.[13]

My point here is to convince you that we cannot apply the same standards to politics that we apply to other social sciences. I think the psychological approach to power is fatally flawed even though I respect the field and admire the scholarship. Speaking as a political scientist, I would say it is very tempting indeed to say, *Where there's smoke there's fire*. I will admit that perhaps power is not as fascinating or as pervasive as I believe. Perhaps I'm a living example of Chadwick's Deficit Theory of Education, proof that political scientists have power hang-ups. But no, power is everywhere. It is real and it is meaningful, and we can feel it whether we can see it or not.[14]

Politics in Three Dimensions

You may dismiss the idea that politics is deeply rooted in human nature, but you would only be deceiving yourself. You may disparage the role of power in society, but this would not alter human nature one iota. All humans share a set of attributes that define the normal range of feeling, thinking, and behaving. Just as a human mother can only give birth to a human baby, your feelings, thoughts, and behaviors form a perfectly accurate representation of human nature. The implication is that your educational and cultural background is a façade, a thin veneer that may change *your* emotional and behavioral repertoire, but does not in any way alter the range of attributes all humans share.

In order to dissuade you from disparaging the role of power in society and deceiving yourself, let us take a step backward. In politics, youth is not a virtue and old age is not a vice. Those of us who majored in political science were compelled to read Plato's *Republic*, which was one of Plato's longest works, and the most influential of the political philosophers who inspired America's founders. In *Republic*, Plato took up the idea of rebirth in his famous Allegory of the Cave, an imaginary tale about a group of cave dwellers who have lived in the same cave since childhood. The Allegory of the Cave is a tale of ignorance and enlightenment, of being and becoming, which also makes a distinction between political realism and the perception of shadows.[15]

The cave dwellers—prisoners, in fact—have chains around their bodies so they cannot stand up and chains around their necks so they cannot turn their heads from side to side. Behind them, there is a fire burning, which casts shadows along the wall. The shadows are puppets and the wall is the screen on which they perform. Some of the shadows on the wall speak, while others do not. Some of the shadows carry tools or other objects, while others do not. Because the prisoners cannot turn their heads, however, they see nothing other than the shadows on the wall in front of them. Furthermore, the cave has an echo, so although the prisoners can converse with one another, they can never be sure whether they are hearing the voice of another prisoner or one of the passers-by.

If this were the only reality the prisoners ever knew it would not take much of a stretch to imagine the kind of culture that would develop around this small society. They would award "best commentator" prizes amongst themselves for those who delivered the most confident predictions about the future, the most malicious insult about the passing shadows, or the most scandalous innuendo. Now, imagine how the typical prisoner would react if you set her free. First, the bright light outside the cave would sting and burn her eyes. Later, when her eyes adjusted to the light, she would be shocked and confused to learn the only reality she knew was nothing but an illusion. Imagine the prisoner's reaction upon seeing three-dimensional objects for the first time—and then the shape of the shadows these objects cast on a wall. How would she respond? Would she perhaps continue to believe the shadows on the wall were more real than the actual objects?

In the face of her persistent denial, is there anything you could do or say to enlighten the former prisoner? One would hope—for the prisoner's sake—she would discard her erroneous beliefs and eventually come around. Imagine again how the prisoner might react if you returned her to the cave and re-chained her next to prisoners who had never been outside the cave. At first, she would be blind in the darkness. Later, perhaps she would try to convince her fellow prisoners the images on the wall were only shadows. Perhaps she would say how much better it is never to leave the safety and certainty of the cave. My point is that understanding human nature, where the laws of politics are rooted, requires objectivity and realism.

In the science-fiction movie *The Matrix* the main protagonist (the character Neo, played by Keanu Reeves) resembles Plato's cave dweller in that he is unaware he lives in a virtual reality. When Neo severs his connection to the Matrix—literally unplugs—he undergoes a kind of rebirth like the prisoner who leaves the cave, and begins to perceive things imperceptible to other cave dwellers. One of the most memorable images in the series is the "digital rain," the computer code, pictograms, and other symbols that scroll down the computer screen like falling rain, and which represents everything in the virtual reality of the matrix. As one character explains, it is easier to read the code than try to keep track of all the activity and all the characters in the simulated world of the Matrix.

Being trapped in the Matrix (or the cave) renders objectivity and realism impossible. Even after being set free, it is still difficult. It takes time to adjust to the brightness, to see the world in three dimensions and develop your *sense of objectivity*. This is part of the transformation process and it is a matter of proper technique. I do not mean to imply everyone has the same potential, any more than everyone can be a world-class athlete or musician. However, people can learn to live up to their own potential. Think of it as a kind of rebirth, but more of a renewal than a reincarnation.

In micropolitics, the sense of objectivity is a key concept. Objectivity refers to the imaginary point of view—the Archimedean Point from Chapter 1—where you would stand if you wanted a perspective uncorrupted by cultural or emotional influences. The opposite of this would be subjectivity, which refers to personal opinions unsubstantiated by facts and (most likely) dominated by beliefs and emotions. Subjectivity implies prejudice, unreliability, and everything contrary to the virtues of objectivity. To label someone's opinion "subjective" is to disparage it.

When I refer to your sense of objectivity, I am referring to your identifications, demands, and expectations. Each of these terms means something in micropolitics. Your identifications are the various categories to which you belong and the groups of which you choose to be a member. Your demands are your desired outcomes, which may be expressed as anything from mild preferences to assertions of inalienable rights. Your expectations are your beliefs about the future, particularly your expectations that the future will be better than the past.[16]

Your sense of objectivity affects the way you learn, the way you communicate with the environment, how you send and receive signals, and how you classify information. Your sense of objectivity also has to do with the movement of your interest and attention, toward objects or toward ideas. Imagine a line from the center of a sphere to its perimeter. In geometry, this is the radius. Now, imagine being able not only to lengthen the radius but also to move the center-point along a spectrum. The larger the radius, the larger your sphere of reference will be. The more mobile the center—toward objects and toward abstract ideas—the greater your mastery of micropolitics will be.

Remember, micropolitics involves close contact with your adversary. The idea of establishing contact in order to penetrate your adversary's psyche highlights an important detail about politics as a social skill: As you master micropolitics, your center of gravity will move. In common usage, the center of gravity is the theoretical point where an object's weight is balanced and evenly distributed. Depending on the shape of the object, this theoretical point may be inside or outside the object's physical body. To push the analogy a little further, enlarging your sense of objectivity will alter your center of gravity.

Remember also that politics is any social relationship that facilitates the control of one human over another. However, making this work requires you to open a door to communicate, establish contact, and penetrate your adversary's psyche in order to gain a sympathetic understanding of his or her circumstances. You must allow the other individual's psyche, which governs the faculty of reason— to come into contact with yours. People have different interests at different times, and the force of your adversary's personality will influence you, and vice versa. This kind of open-door communication illustrates the interactive and responsive aspect of politics, which I mentioned in Chapter 1.

This also relates to the perception of shadows in Plato's Allegory of the Cave. Shadows occupy the space behind an object where light does not reach. Shadows are two-dimensional silhouettes, on the wall of a cave, for example. What if you could increase your sense of objectivity such that shadows were colorful and three-dimensional? It is a mind-boggling concept, but this is how your sense of objectivity subtly dominates your political imagination.

Starting from your perception of shadows and working backward, I would like to introduce two types of people: the introvert and the extrovert.[17] In this context, the introvert and extrovert are not psychological or emotional types, but political types that transcend other demographic categories such as education, gender, class, and culture. When I use the terms *introvert* and *extrovert*, I am not referring to an individual's personality, but specifically to an individual's sense of objectivity. More specifically, I am referring to introverted (subject-oriented) thinking and extroverted (object-oriented) thinking. Each type has its own guiding orientation, which for the introvert is abstract and for the extrovert is concrete.

Anyone who has ever taken the Myers-Briggs Type Indicator (MBTI) should also know that Carl Jung was a pioneer in this field. In Jung's extensive clinical practice, he noticed how some of his patients were more introverted (influenced by their inner selves) while others were more extroverted (influenced by their external surroundings). The concept of introversion versus extroversion, particularly the idea that we all sit somewhere in the middle, along a continuum with these two political types at the polar opposites, is important because politics is, first of all, a social activity. This does not mean someone always and without exception behaves according to type. It means one type predominates. If you accept the possibility of psychological types, however, then you can also accept the possibility of political archetypes, which we will discuss in Chapters 5 and 6.

Generally speaking, the extrovert's sense of objectivity implies a basic orientation toward the external environment, while the introvert's implies a basic orientation toward her own thought processes and emphasizes deference to symbols and a set of inner laws. Extroverts have a greater capacity for social savoir faire and a stronger inclination to act. Extroverts allow themselves to be oriented by experience, while introverts keep the world at a distance. For extroverts, everything begins with experience. For introverts, everything begins with ideas. Extroverts allow themselves to be guided by the external environment, which contains their unconscious projections, and ideas come to them. This is how extroverts organize their thinking.

Introverts have a greater capacity to synthesize ideas and allow themselves be guided by their own ideas, and then impose their thinking on the external environment. Introverts shield themselves from objective influences; they hold themselves in reserve and place ideas (or principles) between themselves and the outside world. For people whose sense of objectivity is introverted, abstractions will occupy the foreground. The chief characteristic of the introverted type is the conscious inner life. The introvert is more than contemplative; the introvert's inner life plays a decisive role. This is how introverts come to understand their experience.

The extrovert sees the introvert's thinking as arbitrary, illogical, and not particularly demanding, while the introvert may see the extrovert's thinking as unimaginative, simplistic, and unsophisticated. Introverts are self-actuated (distinguished by their self-assertion over objects) while extroverts are object-actuated (distinguished by their dependence on objects). According to Carl Jung, the extrovert "makes his presence felt almost involuntarily, because his whole nature goes outwards to the object."[18] Every object and every experience speaks for itself. Whereas ideas can only corrupt the purity of the moment, the object can never have enough value.

Separately, these types have limited utility, but if you can develop the capacity to move along the spectrum toward the object or toward the idea, then you can increase your sense of objectivity. Both types of thinking produce a shadow effect, which reveals the weakness of the other. At their extremes, both of these types risk becoming so formulaic that critical thinking withers away. Everything must fit the formula. Everything must conform to official doctrine regardless of the facts, and anything that does not is (sadly) dismissed as incidental.

We hear about the political spectrum in terms of left-right or liberal-conservative so often that we take it for granted. These types are valid, of course, but have limited utility in micropolitics. Conservatives and liberals alike may be introverted or extroverted. Political introverts may be outgoing and outspoken, while political extroverts may be shy and retiring. If you are an extrovert, it means you have a fundamental preoccupation (like being right- or left-handed) with external determinants and your self-education depends mostly on external data. If you are an extrovert, your psychological activity consists mostly of orienting yourself toward the external environment. The extrovert never strays too far from life. The extrovert does not merely see things as they are, but draws on the external environment as if it were one great big stimulant.

American historian Joseph Ellis alluded to this distinction in his descriptions of George Washington and Thomas Jefferson. Washington was the "rock-ribbed realist" who distrusted visionary schemes and "seductive ideals that floated dreamily in men's minds." Washington's realism was rooted in control over himself, over other people, and over any events he had the power to control, and this put him at the opposite end of the spectrum from Thomas Jefferson, "for whom ideals were the supreme reality and whose inspirational prowess derived from his confidence that the world would eventually come around to fit the pictures he had in his head."[19]

To better understand these types, let me ask a question to help you identify your own type: In general, where do you find the absolutes? Are they in the "real world" proved by science? Or are they found within?[20] What laws govern your behavior? Are they human-made codes of conduct, which correspond to the moral demands of society? Or are they universal laws handed down by God? Where are the absolutes? Your responses to these questions are prerequisites to understanding micropolitics. Your responses will help you understand your own sense of objectivity and help you learn to navigate inward or outward as the situation demands. This will seem intuitive to extroverts, but may be a bit of a reach for introverted types because they bring a particular weakness to the field of micropolitics, which is the tendency to become infatuated with principles, to force facts to support a pet theory and ignore facts that do not.

Even so, each type has tendencies along with challenges that are common to it. Rather than point out the bias or subjectivity of your antagonist/coworker, for example, you should try to be aware of your own type. Self-awareness makes room for growth and thus precedes self-mastery. Self-awareness entails finding the balance (a flexible and elastic balance with a low center of gravity) between introversion and extroversion, between your relation to ideas and your relation to things.

Let me give you an example in which introverts—a lot of introverts—became infatuated with principles, in this case a single principle during the American Civil War when people were outraged that Abraham Lincoln suspended the writ of habeas corpus. The writ of habeas corpus, which comes from English common law, protects people against arbitrary imprisonment. Lincoln ordered the arrest of anyone suspected of giving aid and comfort to the rebels, resisting the draft, discouraging volunteer enlistments, or otherwise obstructing the war effort.

People protested that without habeas corpus, the federal government was no better than a dictatorship, no better than the Confederacy. Lincoln responded with this rhetorical (and mildly sarcastic) question: "Are all the laws, *but one*, to go unexecuted, and the government itself go to pieces, lest that one be violated?"[21] The question is: Where do you find the absolutes? Introverted types are reluctant to sacrifice principle, while extroverted types might sacrifice any and every principle. If you fast-forward to present day, think about which principles you would sacrifice, or which laws you would bend (or break) to combat terrorism. My point is, there is no normal type and no neutral type; only effective or ineffective types based on your personality, your culture, your social environment, and of course your political self-interest.

Along with this liability—the risk of infatuation with principles—introverted types have a clear advantage over extroverted types when it comes to abstract thinking, which is important because the process of abstraction allows people to categorize and to think systematically. People who do not think systematically tend to localize and personalize politics, meaning they blame specific individuals because they do not see the system at work and do not recognize the peculiar logic of politics at work. The process of abstraction begins with a specific real-world problem and then progresses from the specific to the general. By factoring out the details of a problem, you can generalize your thinking, add value to your experience, and stimulate your political imagination.

Extroverts have a habit of looking outside themselves for solutions when they could be looking inward. Part of the problem is the influence of the Internet, movies, and particularly television, which promote voyeurism rather than introspection. However, identifying the two types will not end the conflict between them, nor will identifying your own type. The idea is not to become dependent on one type of thinking, but to adopt the most politically useful aspects of each. You must identify your own type and develop your sense of objectivity (balanced, mobile, and flexible) to avoid obscuring your perception of reality and thus limiting your alternative courses of action.

For further explanation of the differences between the introverted and extroverted types, please refer to the different instrumental values (moral values and competence values) in Chapter 4. Behaving consistently with moral values means behaving honestly and responsibly, which highlights the introvert's deference to abstract principles. Conversely, behaving consistently with competence values means behaving logically and skillfully, which highlights the extrovert's basic orientation toward the "real world."

I was party to a conversation recently in which the topic was the difference between British and American politicians. Someone asked, "What makes a politician?" People chimed in with the usual characteristics: good people skills, good communication skills, good negotiation skills, self-confidence, and a depth and breadth of knowledge relevant to the job. To this I would add the three basic qualifications Aristotle required of all politicians. First was devotion to the rule of law. Second was possession of abilities equal to their office. And third was a sense of justice.[22] I would add love of learning to this list. According to Plato, love of learning was the single most important characteristic of a true leader—and true leaders were as uncommon then as they are now. Those who disliked or had no predisposition for lifelong learning would lack the ability to tell right from wrong, and would have no way of judging a good idea from a bad one. Our cities and states (and our corporations and universities by extrapolation) would never come close to achieving their true potential, said Plato, until philosophers were kings and vice versa—meaning until political greatness came together with wisdom.[23]

In our day and age, the idea of lifelong education, beginning in youth and continuing throughout one's adult life, should be a basic qualification for politicians. What does it mean to combine political greatness and wisdom? What does it mean to suggest that philosophers should lead? Before you respond, remember a philosopher is not just a lover of knowledge but someone who is always curious to learn new things and never satisfied with the status quo. Remember as well that politics is a social affair and that any understanding of micropolitics based entirely on the individual would be incomplete.

Let me tell a story from Plato's *Republic* to illustrate the point. It is a story about a ship's pilot, an honorable man who was taller and stronger than his crew but whose navigational skills were average, and whose eyesight and hearing were both beginning to fail.[24] The crew was constantly fighting with one another about who should steer the ship. Every sailor was of the opinion that he was most qualified, even though his skills were no better than the pilot's skills. They crowded around the pilot, begged and pleaded with him to give them the helm, and threatened to cut to pieces and throw overboard anyone who disagreed. The mutineers promised to reward anyone who helped them take over the ship and to punish anyone who did not. Having failed to make their case, they plotted a mutiny, drugged the pilot, and took possession of the ship by force. They unlocked the storeroom, ate and drank their fill, and continued the voyage in the manner you would expect from a gang of mutineers.

Unfortunately, the mutineers never considered all of the pilot's expertise that seemed superfluous when the water was calm and the sky was blue. The mutineers never considered the pilot's unique job qualifications: being able to read the sky and the water, knowing the stars and the wind, and everything involved with piloting the ship under a wide variety of conditions. They never considered the mystery and mastery that you cannot see from the outside.

This brings us back to our definition of self-mastery from Chapter 1: self-mastery entails the power *to* (the personal element) as well as the power *over* (the social element). The question at the top of this section was, "What makes a politician?" Good people skills, communication skills, and negotiation skills are social elements. Self-confidence, knowledge relevant to the job, devotion to the rule of law, abilities equal to the office, a sense of justice, and a love of learning are personal elements.

The story about the ship's pilot is also interesting because it exemplifies what we might call *the union of authority with the politician's art*. If you look horizontally, you see politics as a competition. If you look vertically, however, you see politics as an exchange between someone who wants power and someone (or a group) who wants to confer that power on someone else. Speaking as a political scientist, I would say this is what makes politics essential because we need politicians, those masterful figures who bring their personal prestige and their social prestige—the power we have vested in them—to our most pressing problems.

This is also why we (in America at least) have term limits because we confer prestige on flawed human beings, people who need an office and a title to compensate for their personal shortcomings. There is something corrosive about this exchange. Somehow, identifying too closely with the crowd convinces people they are absolved of personal responsibility. It corrupts one's moral compass and deadens one's sensitivity to human suffering. I do not want to imply disdain in any way for the political opinions of groups. After all, without a group, there is no power differential, and without this, there is no politics. However, groups can exercise a suggestive force on individuals that is almost irresistible. Fear and hatred are particularly contagious, which explains why the average political opinion of a large group is often at a level below that of an individual. Because politics is interactive and responsive, it is easy to become emotionally involved with the group and taken in by the group's lower and more primitive drives. Plato recognized this inherent tension in human nature—as though there were factions within the soul at war with one another—and saw this reflected in the struggles of different factions within the state. Aristotle came to a similar conclusion. Every human is composed of a body and soul, he said. One is the governor and the other is the governed because one is capable of reason and the other is not.

Just like politics, prestige is an interpersonal situation requiring at least two people: one to claim the honor and one to honor the claim. People will claim prestige for many reasons, including property, birth, occupation, education, and income.[25] And when people honor a claim of prestige, it is necessary to put on a show of deferential behavior.[26] For those who claim it, prestige is very attractive and dangerous for the individual and society alike, because conferring and receiving prestige becomes a habit that neither the recipient nor the society can seem to break. When you give supremacy to someone, you demote yourself and voluntarily relinquish your power, and vice versa: Any office or title you hold signifies the collective approval of society.[27] You represent the office, but the office represents an accumulation of social forces that came into existence through the cooperation of many people.[28]

The Art of the Possible

As stated, politics has its own laws and its own peculiar logic, which distinguishes political behavior from other kinds of social behavior. Furthermore:

1. The laws of politics are rooted in human nature and impervious to our preferences.

2. Politics is about power.

3. Politics is any social relationship that facilitates control of one human over another.

4. Self-interest is the essence of politics.

5. Self-interest is the most reliable standard to judge political action.

6. We can and should judge political action according to the highest ethical standards.

As I have outlined and repeated the "first principles," I do not want to give the impression that anything is possible, nor do I want to give the impression that the world was created yesterday. We were all born into (and continue to work in) a world with vast differences in the distribution of power. Although you may have certain inalienable rights—endowed by your creator, as it were—having a right is not the same as having a skill. A skill is something you acquire by education, training, and experience. Certainly, you can accomplish great things in your organization through politics. History teaches us this lesson, but not without limits.

What limits? The answer comes from another master practitioner of political realism, the Prussian aristocrat and statesman Otto von Bismark, who served as first chancellor of the German Empire. *Die politik ist die kunst des möglichen*, he said. "Politics is the art of the possible." Nobody knows for a fact whether he said this first, but it has been attributed to him for so long that the actual source hardly matters. The point is, politics is not the art of the perfect, but the art of the possible; the art of the next best.

If politics is the art of the possible, then micropolitics is the art of recognizing all the conditions and constraints that make your *first choice* unavailable without losing sight of your *second choice*.[29] This distinction is important because the goal of all political action

is to produce the maximum positive outcome while optimizing allocation of scarce resources and minimizing waste. However, it is
important to define this goal based on accurate assumptions. It is
important to recognize all the conditions, all the constraints, and all
the factors that would make your ideal unrealistic. Once you have
eliminated the false ideal, then you can concentrate on the next-
best solution. This now becomes the true ideal, the new organizing
principle upon which you will formulate and execute your strategy.
This is where having a sense of objectivity that is elastic and mobile
becomes an asset.

In addition to being objective and realistic about human nature
(and this means *your* nature) you need to be objective and realistic
about your situation at the office. How do you know what is realistic? How do you organize and bring discipline to your thinking?
One way is by following a step-by-step process of abstraction, excluding any information outside the political sphere. In this way,
you can develop a systematic and practical arrangement of the facts,
patterns, and interdependencies in the situation, and then you can
ask yourself, *What is the next-best solution?* In this way, you can develop a theory of the case. This is how smart lawyers arrange the
facts and the law in a way that favors their client. Your theory of
the case should be a reproduction of reality—including inconve-
nient facts—and not a work of fiction. It should be abstract but not
imaginary.

Management theorists have called this the "theory-in-use,"
which is the theory that actually governs your actions, as opposed to
your "espoused theory," which is the theory you use to rationalize
or explain your actions.[30] Your theory-in-use is your *hypothesis tested
against observable data*, which consists of your values, strategies, and
assumptions, as well as your standards of success. This is very different from an espoused theory, which is the theory someone communicates to others, announces to the world upon request. When
people keep their intentions and strategies private, they engender
distrust, and perpetuate a culture of distrust. This "tends to reinforce

the disposition of individuals to act according to theories-in-use that feature win/lose behavior and unilateral self-protection."[31] As stated in principle number three (above) no matter how virtuous people may appear in public, very few people are capable of making long-term sacrifices contrary to their interests.

Practicing micropolitics in the workplace requires you to ignore distractions that would weaken your resolve or cause you to swerve. When you are in the thick of it, it is easy to overreact based on a piece of information that later turns out to be meaningless. The challenge is to maintain your ability to think abstractly, read the field, and take in new information as if you were sitting in the comfort of your favorite chair. For example, there is never a shortage of workplace rumors about who is getting promoted, who is on her way out, and who is sleeping with whom. People will talk. And people will talk *about you*. Let it slide, but practice iron self-discipline in your own speech. This doesn't mean don't talk; just make sure there is substance in your words, something real behind the talk. Practicing self-discipline this way will prevent you from overreacting to idle criticism and gossip.

Fortunately, there is a way to read the field, arrange the facts, patterns, and interdependencies in the situation, and develop a theory of the case. Your theory should consist of:

1. your comprehension of the participants in the situation, their roles and expectations, and their competing and complementary goals;

2. the culture, attitudes, values, and beliefs among the participants about right and wrong;

3. the formal or informal boundaries (the turf) that some participants may consider their personal territory or sphere of influence; and

4. the strengths and weaknesses of all participants in the situation (including your own strengths and weaknesses) as well as the degree to which the situation lends itself to personal intervention.[32]

Your arrangement of these facts, patterns, and interdependencies will help you discern the best available solution and decide if initiating or escalating conflict will *improve* your situation.

This depends on developing your *situational awareness*, defined as "the perception of the elements in the environment within a volume of time and space, the comprehension of their meaning, and the projection of their status in the near future."[33] The most important product of situational awareness is the ability to see the abstract beginnings of the future and anticipate change. This implies comprehension of all the elements in the current situation along with anticipation of the future situation—not some distant dream, but the *immediate* future.

First, ask yourself, *What is the degree to which the situation (or environment) lends itself to personal intervention?* **Second**, *What is your position and status?* That is, *Are you strategically placed within the situation?* Note: Your status in an organization isn't the same as your position. It is easy to define your position by your title, office, and place in the hierarchy, but defining your status is harder because it can fluctuate.[34] Defining your status is also harder because status is dependent on other values, such as your intelligence, education, expertise, and reputation. These values won't give you power over others, but they are effective leadership cues. Your status, similar to your prestige, is a reflection of the image others form of you. Status is something you project outward *and* something people confer on you, like the social equivalent of self-esteem. **Third**, ask yourself, *What are your relative strengths and weaknesses—and what are the strengths and weaknesses of other individuals in the situation?* If the situation is unstable such that the actions of a single individual could affect the outcome, then *the variable of skill* becomes very important because the greater your skill, the less dependent you are on the situation being favorable, the less dependent you are on being strategically placed within the situation, and the greater the likelihood your skill (rather than someone else's) will determine the outcome.[35]

The question remains: How do you know what is possible? We are all members of multiple overlapping networks, from households to neighborhoods and beyond. We have jobs, family ties, and other commitments, which constrain the primitive, instinctual element of your nature and limit your freedom. This means micropolitics requires a high degree of sensitivity toward social cues and observation of the effect you have on the world—also known as self-monitoring. If you are a "low" self-monitor, you will often ignore social and interpersonal cues, whereas if you are a "high" self-monitor you will be able to read the field, and learn from and respond to the people around you.[36] Thus, when I remind you that politics is a social affair I am asking you to push your sense of objectivity outward, away from yourself and into social space.

However, when I remind you that the laws of politics are rooted in human nature, I am asking you to push your sense of objectivity downward, toward the cultural and collective elements shared by the entire human species. Masters of micropolitics push outward and downward because the political animal is a social animal as well as a primitive, instinctive animal.[37] As Carl Jung said, "Every individual needs revolution, inner division, overthrow of the existing order, and renewal."[38] And I would like you to pay close attention to Jung's precise chronology: revolution, inner division, overthrow of the existing order, and finally renewal. Nothing in life is immune to change, and politics is no exception. Now is the time for change. Now is the time to leave the cave, unplug from the Matrix, and redefine the political mystique—a task we will undertake in Chapter 3.

Chapter 3

The Political Mystique

There is an old story project managers tell each other. It goes like this: Two project managers receive an assignment to install a concrete walkway through a busy quad. The project managers must first choose from among several routes. A young project manager fresh out of school recommends analyzing patterns and peak times of foot traffic. However, the more experienced project manager recommends simply pouring the concrete where the grass is already worn down to bare dirt.

There is an anti-intellectual lesson to this story, which makes taking sides with the salty veteran almost irresistible. There is also an economic lesson: Pouring the concrete where people have worn the grass away not only saves travel time, but it also saves concrete. There is yet another lesson about the nature of complex systems, which you can infer from the dirt path, which has become a hostile environment for grass. The daily parade of people, the path, and the grassy areas on either side are all elements of a complex and dynamic micro-scale system. The continued existence of this micro-scale system depends on people walking over it to keep the grass from growing back. Finally, there is a lesson in the nature of politics. The path indicates a certain shared habit, a pattern of repetitive behavior without conscious choice. This is how a path becomes a rut and a rut becomes a mystique.

According to German political scientist Karl Loewenstein, "Politics is nothing else but the struggle for power." Loewenstein considered power one of the basic (and often dominant) urges in human nature. However, like many philosophers and political scientists before him, from Aristotle to Machiavelli, Montesquieu to the American founding fathers, Loewenstein analyzed power mostly as a governmental process. He acknowledged the existence of invisible and unofficial power holders but only within a system of political parties, interest groups, and branches of government. Thus, all political power is institutional, official, impersonal, and therefore legitimate.[1] This is the traditional political mystique. And this is the rut that prevents you from seeing that politics takes place wherever there are people—in all kinds of situations, formal and informal. Thus, micropolitics is "social," having to do with human behavior but also "societal," having to do with the systems and structures of human society.[2]

Betty Friedan's *Feminine Mystique* came out in 1963. This book was a milestone in the American women's movement and paved the way for millions of women to have meaningful professional careers, realize their abilities fully, and receive recognition in society beyond marriage and motherhood. Here's the long definition: "The feminine mystique says that the highest and the only commitment for women is the fulfillment of their own femininity. It says that the great mistake of Western culture, through most of its history, has been the undervaluation of this femininity. It says this femininity is so mysterious and intuitive and close to the creation and origin of life that man-made science may never be able to understand it."[3]

In 1969, American author and feminist Carol Hanisch wrote a brief essay called "The Personal is Political," which appeared in an anthology about the women's liberation movement.[4] Hanisch recalled attending many meetings with other feminist leaders back then. Although the meetings were intellectually stimulating—and often went on until long after midnight—they were also therapeutic for Hanisch. In the late 1960s when Hanisch was writing, it was commonplace to attack or dismiss leaders of the feminist movement for airing their "personal problems," such as civil rights, reproductive rights, equal pay, and sex or body image, in public. One lesson Hanisch learned from these meetings and the whole movement is that personal problems are political problems and vice versa.

More than 50 years before Hanisch's landmark essay, however, Carl Jung began his work on psychological types. Jung observed that when someone's "personal problem" coincides with and shares characteristics similar to external events, the personal problem becomes magnified and acquires a dignity it did not have before. Whereas the so-called personal problem is subjective, humiliating, and isolated, a political problem—which is by definition a social problem—is redemptive. This is how the personal becomes the political. As I said in Chapter 1, when you strip away all the dynasties and conquests, all the governments, political parties, and inter-office factions, and reduce politics down to the essentials, nothing could be more personal. And when you think about power in terms of asserting yourself, taking control, and participating in the decisions that affect your life, nothing could be more personal.

Political Structures

The organizing principle of micropolitics is "the personal is political," and vice versa. Although this principle effectively redefines the political mystique and removes arbitrary limitations on the subject, it does not tell us anything specific about the various structures, instruments, systems, and archetypes of micropolitics. In international politics, for example, there is a system of sovereign nation-states and alliances, as well as numerous non-state actors. In national politics, we have a system of political parties, interest groups, branches of government, and federal, state, and municipal jurisdictions. In the modern workplace, we have all the artifacts of corporate bureaucracy, including boards, directors, shareholders, suppliers, customers, beleagured employees, and—seemingly straight out of the brilliant comic strip *Dilbert* by Scott Adams— incompetent managers, know-it-all consultants, and cubicles as far as the eye can see. Does micropolitics have systems and structures analogous to national and international politics?

I would say yes, and therefore, we should not limit our understanding of politics to federal, state, or local governments, political parties, and lobbyists. We must redefine the political mystique to include relationships with your boss, coworkers, friends, and family members. If we agree with the premise that situations are politicized when power is introduced, then any relationship and any organization may become political.[5] According to two prominent management theorists, "Before an organization can be anything else, it must be *political*."[6] This is a bold assertion, which I believe to be true, but we should test this assertion by changing it into a question.

Must an organization be political before it can be anything else? Let's start with the most imperfect and impermanent institution in human society: the mob. I consulted the dictionary and discovered it was fashionable in 17th-century English to shorten long words or phrases to one syllable. Thus, the mob is an abbreviation of the Latin phrase *mobile vulgus*, which literally means "the excitable populace." In modern English, the mob is a fickle crowd, an unruly crowd, and, hundreds of years later, the word still carries the same tone of contempt. If politics is about power, and social relationships become politicized when power is introduced, then a mob qualifies for the purposes of micropolitics.

What about more formal organizations at the other end of the spectrum? That's an easier question because in a formal organization, office-holders such as CEOs are representatives of the organization. Individuals make decisions and take action as agents of the organization. In order for this to take place, there must be permanence, there must be rules, and there must be some delegation of authority because there is a distinction between individuals and the official roles they play. Organizations consist of competing factions, and in order to understand their behavior, we must understand the nature of conflict, the distribution of power among the factions, and the way conflict is resolved, through negotiation and compromise or domination and submission.[7] Establishing the idea that all kinds of organizations—from the most primitive, unofficial group of people to the most complex Fortune-500 company—are fundamentally political is an important step toward understanding the systems and structures of micropolitics.

I said earlier that I wanted to strip away all the dynasties and conquests, all the governments, political parties, and factions, and reduce politics down to the essentials. One of the essential structures of micropolitics is the family, which may not qualify as a "formal organization," but is the basic social structure for organizing essentials such as shelter, safety, and security, and which also is the basic economic structure for the production, distribution, and consumption of resources. This essential structure arises from the depths of human nature and then becomes something we can see and feel as we live together, eat together, share resources, and raise children.[8]

Is the family, as I have described it, consistent with the claim that an organization must be political before it can be anything else? Is a family made up of factions? I would say yes. Is power distributed among competing factions? Again, I would say yes. Is there conflict? Sometimes there is. Does the conflict result in domination and submission, or negotiation and compromise? I would say yes, yes, yes, and sometimes yes. If you gave different responses to these questions, perhaps it indicates you have a more introverted orientation, and a more idealized idea of the family.

Regardless, by reducing politics down to the essentials and excluding information outside the political sphere, you can develop a systematic (and practical) arrangement of the facts, patterns, and interdependencies in the situation. This will help you recognize all the conditions and constraints that make your first choice unavailable without losing sight of your second choice. This is what makes politics the art of the possible: recognizing that your first choice is unavailable without losing sight of your second choice. This is not the art of the perfect, but the art of the second-best. This helps you redefine the political mystique according to the standards *you* set, not someone else. Perhaps this will help you better understand the different instruments of power, which we will explore in the next section.

Power Instruments

As stated, there is a difference between personal power (the power *to* or the power *of*) and social power (the power *over* someone or something).[9] Although both concepts of power are valid, one is political and the other is not. Because politics is a social affair, the *power over* is particularly relevant to micropolitics.

Based on this distinction, we can identify different instruments of power using terminology developed by Canadian-American economist John Galbraith.[10] The first instrument is "condign," which is a fancy term for "appropriate" or "well-deserved." Condign power implies the ability to force someone's submission and alter her behavior by offering her a sufficiently unpleasant alternative with adverse consequences. Essentially, condign power is the stick, which wins submission via threat, intimidation, or coercion. The second instrument is compensatory power, which implies the ability to alter someone's behavior by offering a reward—the carrot. In our contemporary system, rewards such as promotions, public recognition, and money (or other valuables) are effective instruments to alter someone's behavior.

The carrot and the stick are instruments of the "power elite," a term coined by American sociologist C. Wright Mills.[11] The power they enjoy in their various roles is "ex officio," meaning authority or power by virtue of their status, office, position, wealth, or family ties. Not everyone agrees with Mills, or at least not everyone agrees to the stipulations necessary to believe the power elite theory. One sociologist listed these stipulations as follows: First, the power elite represent a very small minority compared to "the vast army" of middle managers you would normally meet. Second, the power elite share a homogeneous worldview; members may disagree with one another about details but they don't doubt the worldview. Third, the power elite have no countervailing force, and as we know from the tension of opposites there is always a countervailing force necessary to maintain the natural equilibrium of all complex systems, including social and political systems.[12]

Another author was skeptical of the concept of class power. He said the whole idea of the power elite was fallacious and anybody who disagreed with him was living in "a twilight zone."[13] However, the same author listed five laws of power relevant to our understanding of micropolitics:

1. Power fills a vacuum in any organization.

2. Power is invariably personal.

3. Power is invariably based on a system of ideas.

4. Power is exercised through and depends on institutions.

5. Power and responsibility constantly interact.

Although it is practically impossible to overestimate the importance of money and organization as sources of power in society, especially for those who aspire to the C-suite, authentic leadership does not come from the corner office. People entirely dependent on ex officio power should learn to become less dependent because they may never earn recognition as a leader beyond the narrow confines of their office or title. That is, people may "salute the uniform" and may continue to do so as long as you wear the uniform. However, there is a big difference between these showy bureaucratic formalities and the kind of personal respect people only feel for authentic leaders.

All organizations have structures where power is vested, and instruments to facilitate control. In the American government, the Constitution establishes different branches with distinct roles and a system of checks and balances to minimize the concentration of power.[14] Although the president serves as chief executive, the constitution delineates her lawful powers. Legislators, judges, cabinet secretaries, and other political appointees all have bureaucratic authority in one form or another. In large private-sector companies, the power is vested in the chief executive officer, who works under the general supervision of a board of directors representing the shareholders. The distribution of power is concentrated, not symmetrical, and not democratic.

In many universities, the chief executive officer also works under the general supervision of a board, but there is also "shared governance," meaning power is distributed among faculty members, administrators, and trustees. Faculty members help govern the institution and take part in personnel decisions, budgeting, and a variety of policy issues. Regardless of the structure—whether power is concentrated or widely distributed—those with the best political skills will exert the most power. There is always a boss—someone with bureaucratic authority—but the boss may or may not be the most powerful individual in the organization, depending on her political skills.

The lesson here is that politics is not the sole prerogative of people who belong to a class or who exercise bureaucratic authority. This means you—and anyone else employed in any kind of organization—need to enhance your political skills. This is what makes Galbraith's third instrument of power—conditioned power—a subject of great practical importance, especially for those of us who are not members of the "power elite." Conditioned power implies the ability to alter someone's behavior by changing—literally conditioning—their belief system through persuasion or education. Conditioned power is distinct from condign or compensatory because the subject may or may not make a conscious choice to accept the reward or avoid the punishment. Thus, the effects of a conditioned or learned response are more gradual but also more durable than condign or compensatory power.

I want to reinforce the idea that politics does not necessarily require coercion or the use of force. The instruments of power range from total domination (in the form of threats and rewards) to the gentlest suggestion (in the form of education, propaganda, and persuasion).[15] These informal controls are examples of conditioned power, the purpose of which (according to Galbraith) is "the contented submission to the will of others."[16] Conditioned power is so subtle that most people are unaware it is being applied, but once you pass a certain threshold—the tipping point, as Malcolm Gladwell famously called it—conditioned power is very low-maintenance. For example, with enough familial conditioning, children will obey their parents; with enough religious conditioning, people will submit to the teachings of their church; with enough political conditioning, people will respect the authority of their leaders; with enough market conditioning, consumers will buy the products that advertisers claim will bring them health, wealth, happiness, and sex appeal. These categories (familial, religious, political, and market) are systems and structures. That is, they are made up of contending parties, and power is distributed among the parties. There is conflict, which sometimes results in dominance and submission, or negotiation and compromise.

To understand the instrument of conditioned power, it is necessary to understand the role of culture in human systems/structures. Culture is cumulative symbolic learning, which passes among members of a community and from generation to generation. Culture is also a problem-solving tool based on trial-and-error learning to help the community adapt to its environment. Finally, culture is a belief system, which reflects the values of the community.[17] When we combine and consolidate these three elements, the result is this: Culture is a set of attitudes, values, and behaviors shared by a community, which are passed from generation to generation, and which are based on trial-and-error learning. This definition is useful (and necessary) to understand conditioned power: the slow, relentless process that trains people to act or respond in ways "approved" by society. This kind of conditioning is the process of acquiring (and un-acquiring) values and beliefs that influence your behavior. This process begins in childhood, continues through adulthood, and is so powerful that it is impossible for you to receive signals from the environment without those signals passing through the filter of your own culture.[18]

To demonstrate the subtle influence of cultural conditioning (not necessarily conditioned power, but the importance of contextual and situational awareness) let me share a personal anecdote. On the Fourth of July 1982, a few months after I graduated from college, I landed in Libreville, Gabon (West Africa), to begin my two-year service as a Peace Corps volunteer. Removed from my familiar environment, I made an effort to adapt to my host country and live in harmony with the local culture. After the disorientation and culture shock subsided, my cultural immersion and isolation taught me how to differentiate between myself and the conventions of my Southern California upbringing. Layer after layer of cultural veneer began to peel away throughout a period of weeks and months. I came away with a slightly better understanding of Gabonese culture and a much deeper understanding of my own.

It is hard to explain why this happens to some people and not others. I have observed this process of differentiation and self-awareness not only in many Peace Corps volunteers but also in many students who have recently returned from studying in a foreign university, but almost never in tourists or business travelers. There is something unique and very powerful—though not foolproof—about this kind of experience, which is a result of *consciously* living and working in another culture for an extended time. We will dig deeper into this topic of differentiating between yourself and the group and reacquainting yourself with parts of your personality—also known as individuation—in Chapter 4.

Back to the story: My assignment was to build a primary school in a remote village called Obouo (pronounced "oh-BOO-oh"), located in the southeastern part of the country, near the Congolese border. My construction crew consisted of six Pygmy villagers. We made our bricks by hand and dried them in the sun. We used no power tools on the site, but we did have a beaten-up four-wheel-drive Toyota pickup truck. One day in November 1982, I woke to the sound of rain pounding on my roof. I looked at the clock: 5:30 a.m., which is when the roosters usually woke me up. I was half hoping it would keep raining, but it let up by about 7:30, the time my crew would normally arrive and we would get to work. When I arrived at the construction site, however, none of the workers had arrived. I waited 20 minutes or so, and then decided to go looking for them.

The construction site was located on the main road through the village, but my crew members all lived in a cluster of small houses up a hill about a mile away. To get there, you followed a rutted clay road that marked the boundary between the rain forest and the plateau. Before I left my house, the thought occurred to me that I would make better time if I jogged. Because it rained hard all night long, I anticipated the clay road would be nearly impassable, even with four-wheel drive. I changed into my running shorts, and started up the hill. As I jogged along, I said *bon jour* to the women carrying heavy loads of firewood slung on their backs. I greeted the children on their way to the crumbling old schoolhouse across the road from the construction site where we were building the new school. As I neared the Pygmy village, I saw more children peeking around the corner, who squealed when they saw me and scurried away. By the time I arrived, it seemed the whole village had turned out to greet me. I asked to speak with the village chief, and told him I was having problems with the workers—they were not coming to work.

One by one, they all came out of their huts. Apparently, they had the same idea I had; they were hoping it would keep raining too. The chief scolded them, and I challenged them to a race back down the hill to the construction site. They all agreed to come to work, but only one (his name was Gilbert) took up the challenge to run with me. Because he was barefooted, I did not think Gilbert had a chance, but he took off sprinting and was soon ahead of me by about 25 yards. Then, he started to walk. I kept jogging at my usual pace and soon caught up to him, so he started sprinting again, and again was soon ahead of me by about 25 yards. He did this several times, each time sprinting, tiring out and walking, and each time laughing and smiling when I caught up to him, but pride forced him to start running again.

Soon we rounded the corner and the construction site came into view, and we both started sprinting. I mean we were really running—like the stragglers in front of the bulls at Pamplona. I had too much energy left for Gilbert to keep up and I beat him by a few yards. Now, I want you to freeze this picture in your mind: I am in shorts and shoes (with that little swoosh) running, grimacing, with arms outstretched. Gilbert is in ragged clothes and barefooted, running, grimacing, and carrying a machete. Did I not mention that detail? In the Gabonese countryside, men carried machetes all the time to cut firewood or kill snakes. In addition to freezing this picture, I would like you to forget the back story, all the events leading up to this scene, and all the personal details affecting my and Gilbert's motivations and reactions. Now, tell me what you see.

As I said earlier, politics is a social affair requiring sustained contact with your social milieu, which implies a high level of interdependence between you and your environment, and as I said in Chapter 2, your sense of objectivity affects the way you learn, the way you communicate, and how you send and receive signals. Like your sense of objectivity, cultural conditioning subtly (or not so subtly) dominates your perception and influences your ability to read the field. Without knowing any of the back story, my guess is that you probably saw a barefooted Pygmy brandishing a large machete running as fast as he can chasing a white man. You might reasonably assume the white man said or did something wrong, but without knowing the back story, you would probably never guess Gilbert and I were friends and colleagues.

Let me give you another example to demonstrate the subtle influence of contextual understanding. A few years ago, I saw an interesting public service announcement (PSA) while I was riding on the London Underground. There were advertisements posted above the windows running the length of the car, but one in particular caught my eye. It was a black-and-white photograph of what appeared to be a white policeman (in uniform) chasing a black man. I say "appeared" because the purpose of this PSA was to raise awareness of subliminal racism. In fact, the photo was cropped, and both men in the photo were police officers; the white officer was in uniform and the black officer was in plain clothes, and both of them were chasing someone else outside the frame. I liked this PSA so much I wanted to tear it down and take it home, but it was rush hour and the subway car was full. Nonetheless, this PSA is memorable for two reasons. First, it highlights the importance of your theory-in-use (which consists of your values, strategies, assumptions, and standards of success). Second, this PSA illustrates the effects of cultural conditioning. The less you know about the back story, the more likely you are to ignore, devalue, or misinterpret the facts based on your cultural conditioning.

The ability to resist conditioned power begins with recognizing that the old mystique is nothing but an arbitrary and artificial relic, and then changing your perceptions of reality. The ability to internalize authority and redefine the mystique (including the feminine mystique of the mid-20th century) is evidence of your autonomy.[19] Perhaps it goes without saying, but women have an additional burden that men do not when it comes to overcoming conditioned power. Betty Friedan called this process "progressive dehumanization," which refers to purposely contrived conditions that force prisoners to surrender their human identity, adopt child-like behavior, and slowly "adjust" to the conditions of a concentration camp. The capacity for self-determination is systematically destroyed along with all hope that the future is going to be any better. This is a gradual process that occurs in imperceptible stages. At the end, however, the process of progressive dehumanization is complete.[20]

American author and linguist Suzette Haden Elgin also explored this topic in *The Gentle Art of Verbal Self-Defense*. If you are a woman living in any culture dominated by men, or a member of any other category in which there may be a bias against you, then you have probably received a lifetime's worth of conditioning (or progressive dehumanization). For women living in a male-dominated culture, this conditioning begins in infancy and lives on in nursery rhymes and picture books. Even though this conditioning follows women through Sunday school and high school, to college and marriage, it is still possible, and even common, for women to convince themselves they are totally free from any of the effects of cultural conditioning.[21]

This is one of the peculiar characteristics of conditioned power. Often, the players in the drama are unaware of what is happening. We willingly submit to authority and we recognize certain behaviors as "normal" because of conditioned power, whether it comes in the form of education, cultural transmission, or the slow drip-drip of television advertising delivered in daily doses throughout a lifetime. Conditioned power is subtly effective for perpetuating religious doctrine, for winning submission to military policy, and for extolling the virtues of fascism, socialism, capitalism, and every other system of political economy.

Complex Systems

Along with the structures and instruments of politics (and later the archetypes) it is necessary to understand complex systems. This may seem unnecessary, like an expensive tool you rarely use that sits at the bottom of your toolbox. In this instance, however, complexity is not the opposite of simplicity. There is no way to simplify the principles of complex systems without distorting them. And so now I am asking you to trust me when I say you need this tool to master micropolitics.

American political scientist Robert Dahl defined a political system as "any persistent pattern of human relationships that involves, to a significant extent, power, rule, or authority." He listed the four characteristics of a system:

1. It must be abstracted specifically for the purpose of analysis.

2. It must have boundaries, and you must be able to determine what lies within the system and what lies outside those boundaries.

3. A system may be an element (or subsystem) of a larger system.

4. A system may be an element of one or more larger systems with minimal overlap.

Points 3 and 4 are important because political science belongs to the social sciences, and political behavior is a specific kind of social behavior, which means any political system is a subsystem of a larger social system.[22]

It might help if you think about systems the way you think about symbols, except in reverse. If a symbol is something visible and/or tangible (such as a flag, a uniform, or a trademark) that represents something abstract, then a system is the opposite. A system is something abstract that represents something concrete, the way a map represents an actual place. However, none of this will make sense—not the systems, not the symbols, not the structures—without a theory. If you don't have a theory, and you copy a successful example without understanding why it was successful, the feedback you receive will be meaningless. If you don't have a theory, there is nothing to learn and your experience has no meaning.[23]

In micropolitics, many of the most critical moments may appear—to the untrained eye—to be insignificant details. But not all details are equal. Some details may appear to be small and trivial, but are part of a system and a chain of consequences that multiplies over time and produces an accumulation of effects. As the proverb goes, "For want of a nail the shoe was lost. For want of a shoe, the horse was lost. For want of a horse, the rider was lost. For want of a rider, the battle was lost. For want of the battle, the kingdom was lost."

In micropolitics, success often depends on recognizing patterns, relationships, and interdependencies. For example, I have been teaching my daughter to play chess, and sometimes she has gotten frustrated because I do not let her win, even when I sacrifice my queen to start the game. We bought a book called *How to Beat Your Dad at Chess*, which offers some insights about how chess masters think, and which also sheds light on micropolitics. Sometimes, chess masters lapse into long periods of concentration before making a move. Other times, they appear to think for a few seconds before moving. This analytical process is directly related to *pattern recognition*, which is helpful for seeing the structures, instruments, and systems of politics.

If you, like the chess master, can recognize similar patterns, positions, or situations you have encountered in the past, it is possible to apply similar tactics to the situation at hand.[24] Micropolitics, like chess, is a combination of one-time calculation and general pattern recognition, and as you increase your self-mastery, the ratio between the two will change. In the beginning, the ratio will be 80 percent one-time calculation and 20 percent general pattern recognition. As your mastery increases, this ratio will reverse, and eventually your ability to recognize patterns will continue to develop until everything you see fits into one big pattern called "complexity."

That is not to say complex systems always behave in ways that are easy to recognize. Sometimes, their behavior is directional and irreversible (children grow up). Sometimes their behavior is cyclical and the flow of events is rhythmic (seasons change), even though we may never see the beginning or the end of the cycle. Any event may produce consequences that are delayed or indirect, but neither the causes nor the effects are arbitrary (one thing leads to another). Causes may be located at any time and in any location in the system, but the effects may be far removed in time and space (the delayed reaction). For these reasons, it is useful to have a well-developed sense of objectivity, specifically because it improves the way you communicate with the environment. The environment is always communicating and sending feedback, which may be extremely complicated, and may appear to be random, but not if you can recognize the patterns.

When I look at the world, I see *a network of mutuality* consisting of an infinite number of systems within subsystems with no floor or ceiling.[25] This vast network is shaped like a three-dimensional lattice with decentralized power nodes and communication channels. Within this network, the systems and subsystems are shaped like a funnel, with centralized power nodes and hierarchical communication channels. Every system within this network behaves according to an identical set of principles. This consistency of adherence both permits and promotes interdependence with other systems.

Because of this interdependence, systems respond to any situation or external stimulus that disturbs their normal condition. Sometimes, systems respond by absorbing the change temporarily and acclimatizing temporarily, but if the disturbance goes on long enough systems will evolve and adjust their behavior irreversibly. When this happens, systems engage in "emergent" behavior. They engage in new behaviors beyond their former capacity and beyond the capacity of their elemental subsystems. Each successive level of evolution increases the system's behavioral repertoire and relative autonomy, and produces greater capacity for self-reflection and consciousness.

It is breathtaking to behold. However, within this magnificent network of mutuality, there is tension, disorder, and chaos. People are not angels, harmoniously coexisting simply because they live together under the same roof, work in the same organization, or attend the same place of worship. People are full of internal conflict—some more than others—and they may respond to conflict with a range of defense mechanisms. For example, some may attribute character traits or emotions to someone else (projection). They may transfer reactions from the original object to something more acceptable (displacement). They may split something into two extreme representations (idealization). Or they may assimilate the character traits of someone else (identification). As I said in Chapter 1, you must recognize your own human nature so you can recognize it in others, and vice versa. Understanding the principles of complexity improves pattern recognition, and vice versa.

People are full of conflict and people are political animals. Each one has a special interest, an entitlement, or an investment at stake. Sometimes these interests are compatible, but mostly they are not. This competition is perfectly consistent with human nature and the laws of complex systems, including social and political systems. As we discussed in Chapter 2, there are two types of learning behavior in micropolitics: introverted (subject-oriented) thinking, which is anticipatory and enables you to preempt or induce environmental change; and extroverted (object-oriented) thinking, which is experiential and adaptive, and enables you to respond to change in the environment by absorbing it. Complex systems induce change and respond to change in much the same way.

However, complex systems also *manage* change, form new structures, and engage in new behaviors without undoing the system's cohesion. Systems regulate themselves naturally by receiving feedback from the environment, and respond to environmental variation by absorbing it. (In the vernacular of complexity, the environment consists of all the conditions external to the system that may affect the functioning of the system.) Object-oriented learning (analogous to the extroverted type) enables systems to learn through experience by observing the consequences of their actions, and then adjust their behavior accordingly. The consequences of this behavior may be far removed in time and space, however, so this process is effective only if the feedback is timely and clear. Subject-oriented learning (analogous to the introverted type) is the opposite. It is creative and instinctive. The system "feeds forward" to preempt environmental variation. This enables the system to function even when feedback from the environment is delayed, unclear, or nonexistent.

Communication with the environment is one of the processes that enables systems to function the way biological organisms metabolize organic nutrients to produce energy and sustain life. This process allows systems to grow and reproduce, maintain their structures, and respond to the environment. I use the word *allow* with some hesitation because without these processes the system becomes rigid and stops growing. With this rigidity comes the inability to send and receive signals. The system may not disintegrate immediately, but it will undergo elaborate contortions to rationalize new information, explain away the anomalies, and continue functioning.

Complexity is part of the structure of politics, and understanding complexity is very helpful (indispensable, you might say) for understanding the patterns and interdependencies in a situation. Another part is the oppositional structure of political relationships, also known as the tension of opposites. The tension of opposites plays an important function in micropolitics and illustrates the principle of differentiation and polarity within a complex system. Jung was almost poetic in his description of the tension of opposites: "Everything young grows old, all beauty fades, all heat cools, all brightness dims, and every truth becomes stale and trite."[26] Elsewhere, Jung issued this warning: "Every archetype contains the lowest and the highest, evil and good, and is therefore capable of producing diametrically opposite results."[27] We will explore archetypes in Chapters 5 and 6, but for now, note that Jung says "everything," not "almost everything," which indicates how pervasive the tension of opposites is.

The tension of opposites (also known as deep binary structure or binary opposition) is the motive power of human evolution.[28] Karl Marx and Friedrich Engels recognized the tension of opposites (based on class, nationality, and religion) in their *Communist Manifesto*. Sigmund Freud recognized this tension in the fundamental hostility between individuals and modern civilization.[29] French writer and philosopher Albert Camus recognized this in his discourse about the rebellious element in human nature. "Power opposes other forms of power," Camus wrote. "It arms and rearms because others are arming and rearming."[30] And Austrian economist Josef Schumpeter recognized the tension of opposites when he coined the phrase "creative destruction" to describe the role of entrepreneurship in a market economy and the evolutionary process of economic change essential to capitalism.[31]

In social situations and interpersonal relations at the office, the tension of opposites with competing interests can be positive and transformative when it pushes development forward. Recall Bill Clinton's tactic of triangulation, which frustrated Clinton's political opponents by appropriating some nominally conservative ideas. On the surface, triangulation appears expedient, if not unprincipled—a criticism anyone could make about any political tactic. However, if you look at triangulation not as a cynical ploy, but as part of the natural order, you can see there is no middle way without polarity. While people (or factions) are busy having a left-right argument, it is possible to withdraw energy from the opposing extremes and direct it toward the middle way. Thus, the divergence of opposing forces produces a convergence at a forward point, or at a higher level. This is *the redemptive middle way*, which uses the tension of opposites to produce change.

All systems depend on the tension of opposites, without which they could not function. This natural polarity is where political conflict originates, and explains why politics requires at least two oppositional people. Opposition is what makes politics necessary. Without opposition, there would be nothing to bump up against, no adversity to overcome. Within this structural conflict, however, lies the hidden spark of regeneration. Although a certain amount of political conflict is inevitable due to the natural bipolarity, systems tend to avoid extremes in favor of sustainable equilibrium.

And this is how complex systems—including political systems—modernize, reproduce, and evolve. Opposing forces and competing influences may push the system out of equilibrium for a while, but eventually the system pushes back. This process of differentiation and self-determination is similar to the process of political individuation, which we will explore in Chapter 4.

Chapter 4

The Inward Journey

In Chapter 3, we examined the structures, instruments, and systems of micropolitics. Before that, at the end of Chapter 2, I asked you to push your sense of objectivity outward and downward. At the risk of contradicting myself, I would like to remind you that every individual needs to fight and win the revolution within. Conversations about power and politics often turn into discussions about how we have to change or how other people have to change. To be sure, the revolution begins with you. But let's not talk about that, at least for now. Let's talk about human nature and human society instead. This is where the laws of politics are rooted and this is where your inward journey begins.[1]

Understanding the laws and structures of politics, the instruments of power, and the principles of complex systems are all important steps on this journey to master micropolitics in the office. As we proceed, we must also be as objective and realistic as possible when it comes to human nature and the primitive, instinctive political animal, even though it may be hiding behind a façade of civilization and cubicle walls and buried under layers of modernity. Part of the challenge is getting close enough to discover what Harold Lasswell called "unrecognized factors present in the personality."[2] These "unrecognized factors" are hidden behind a wall that separates your conscious from your unconscious mind, and in general, there is nothing in your life about which you are so ignorant as your own unconscious mind.[3]

Carl Jung likened this process of self-exploration to someone mistakenly believing she is digging a well when she is actually uncovering a volcano.[4] So, if we're taking an inward journey and perhaps starting a revolution, we'll need a good guide book, preferably written by people who've been there and done that. I can think of none better than *The Federalist Papers*, the series of essays written in the late 18th century by Alexander Hamilton, James Madison, and John Jay to generate support for the U.S. Constitution, which was then awaiting ratification. What makes *The Federalist Papers* relevant for practitioners of micropolitics is the authors' view of human nature *as it is*, without either flattering its virtues or exaggerating its vices. Hamilton, Madison, and Jay cataloged a long list of human failings small and large: avarice, conceit, obstinacy, revenge, vanity, thirst for glory, the ambitious aims of those who indulged in magnificent schemes of personal aggrandizement, *and many other motives not more laudable than these.*

Let's start with No. 76, written by Hamilton: "The supposition of universal venality in human nature is little less an error in political reasoning than the supposition of universal rectitude."

Ah, what a divine gift is the English language, the native tongue of Shakespeare, Milton, and Shaw. *Venality* is one of those words appropriated from Latin by way of French, and it means "for sale." Venality is the susceptibility to bribery, the all-too-human weakness for corruptibility and the willingness to betray one's position of public trust—for a price.

Building on this supposition of universal venality, Hamilton made the argument (in No. 79) for an independent judicial branch, and said, "In the general course of human nature, a power over a man's subsistence amounts to a power over his will." In practice, this means providing a generous salary and lifetime tenure to federal judges to minimize the potential for corruption and immunize judges from political influence. In micropolitics, this merely reinforces one of Morgenthau's principles about the laws of politics being rooted in human nature. Because politics is about power, and because self-interest is the essence of politics, sacrificing one's interests runs contrary to human nature. As stated, this does not mean there are no examples of sacrifice in human history. Rather, it means very few people are capable of this kind of unselfish behavior in the long term because very few are capable of outrunning their own human nature.

In perhaps the most famous passage in *The Federalist Papers*, James Madison asked rhetorically, what is government, if not the greatest reflection of human nature? If people were angels, Madison said, no government would be necessary (No. 51). Perpetual rivalry, competition, and turf wars were perfectly natural, according to Hamilton, and it was not difficult for him to account for this tendency. "It has its origin in the love of power. Power controlled or abridged is almost always the rival and enemy of that power by which it is controlled or abridged" (No. 15). Hamilton also believed it was a general principle of human nature that people were interested in whatever they possessed in proportion to how tightly or how loosely they held it (No. 71). Translation: The longer or harder someone holds on to an office or title (political privilege, interest, entitlement, and so on) the more attached she becomes. Finally, Hamilton said it was a fact of human nature that affections were weaker in proportion to the distance of the object (No. 17). Translation: Events nearby are more important than events far away, which explains why people are more attached to their family than to their neighborhood, and more attached to their neighborhood than to their government.

Hamilton said you should always take into account "the ordinary depravity of human nature" (No. 78), and he was not alone in this assessment. Madison also said there is a "degree of depravity" in human nature that required constant vigilance (No. 55). One reason why Madison and other founders insisted on the separation of powers (and this includes the Establishment Clause of the first amendment) is that they knew the dark side of human nature. The founders wanted to ensure the government would always protect religious freedom, for example, and never establish an official state religion. In this respect, the founders were speaking not just among themselves but also to future generations.[5] They knew someday there would be religious fundamentalists among us who would confuse their will with God's will, and try to impose their religious doctrine. Knowing human nature as they obviously did, the founders were right to be vigilant.

Madison believed "the latent causes of faction" were inherent in human nature, which provides a little more insight regarding the tension of opposites from Chapter 3. Throughout Madison's career, he observed the tendency of people to divide themselves into factions—zealous and mutually hostile factions. The most common rationale for this behavior had to do with the unequal distribution of wealth. The "haves" and the "have-nots" formed their own groups based on their interests in society. In response to this natural tendency to break into factions, the founders decided it was necessary to break up the functions of government, and separated the executive, legislative, and judicial branches. Federalism is another method the American founders employed to break up the functions of government. Federalism governs relations between authorities at various levels and says (in the Bill of Rights) that any and all power not expressly delegated to the federal government belongs to the states or to the people. Thus, according to James Madison (No. 51), "ambition [is] made to counteract ambition," and the abuse of power is checked.

However, the unequal distribution of wealth was not the only pretext Madison observed. In No. 10 he said, "So strong is this propensity of mankind to fall into mutual animosities, that where no substantial occasion presents itself, the most frivolous and fanciful distinctions have been sufficient to kindle their unfriendly passions and excite their most violent conflicts." Madison also said, "The history of almost all the great councils and consultations held among mankind for reconciling their discordant opinions, assuaging their mutual jealousies, and adjusting their respective interests, is a history of factions, contentions, and disappointments, and may be classed among the most dark and degraded pictures which display the infirmities and depravities of the human character" (No. 37). That is to say, discord, jealousy, and depravity are so strong in human nature that people will split into factions for any reason, or for no reason at all.

If you think about all the human excesses the authors of *The Federalist Papers* attempted to check, balance, or expressly prohibit through the power of government, it is possible to see the same dark side of human nature. In the pre-psychoanalytic era when Hamilton, Madison, and Jay were writing, they would have been unfamiliar with Carl Jung's and Sigmund Freud's ideas about human behavior and the unconscious mind.[6] However, they would have been very familiar with Greek literature and the story of Pandora's Box. In case your knowledge of Greek mythology is rusty, Pandora's father, Zeus, gave her a box (sort of a birthday present), but he ordered her not to open it under any circumstances. Curiosity got the better of her, however, and when Pandora opened the box she let out all the evils that afflict us today.

The supposition of universal venality is pessimistic, but is it false? Political theories are always pessimistic—and always should be pessimistic—about human nature and the future of human society.[7] If you disagree—that is, if you think the founders were too pessimistic and that human nature is basically good—then I want you to try something. Visit any Website where readers' comments are unfiltered and unmonitored, such as a daily news blog. Click on a story—any story—related to politics, and read the comments. Regardless whether the story is benign or controversial, you will often find the comments section full of bitterness, hatred, anger, vulgarity, and threats of violence. In this instance, however, I want you *not* to pass judgment, but just observe. If a story has a reasonable number of comments, let us say a hundred or so, I think you can make a reasonable (though not scientific) estimation about the average person.

Keep in mind what I said in Chapter 2, that political types transcend demographic categories such as education, gender, class, and culture. Also keep in mind that this Internet-based sample is probably a little above average in terms of intelligence and education, and a little below average in terms of age. Are you shocked at how quickly people turn into trolls, and how quickly exchanges between readers are reduced to personal insults and threats? If you have noticed this before (and of course you have) then perhaps you already agree that the authors of the *Federalist Papers* were fairly objective and realistic in their assessment of human nature.

If you still need convincing, let me share what psychologist James Hillman had to say when he explained what it really means to be human. To be human is to be loving and forgiving. And to be human is to be violent and vengeful, cowardly and cruel. The hand that rocks the cradle is also the hand that tosses the grenade and holds the flame-thrower. "Hitler was human, and Stalin too, and the soldiers banging at Christ's legs were as human as their victim, and they knew what they were doing."[8] Even if we ignore history on our inward journey, and instead choose to concentrate on contemporary events, we must not neglect or distort the meaning of the word *human*.

The Collective Element

In Chapter 3, we discussed the powerful influence of cultural conditioning, which profoundly affects your perceptions and hinders your ability to recognize (and redefine) the political mystique. There is another systemic force at work in politics, analogous to cultural conditioning but which functions at a deeper level. This is "collective conditioning" and it represents the onslaught of prelogical human instinct. To access the collective element, you must descend into the undifferentiated mass of humanity. At this depth, you are not an individual being. There is no individuality, no independence, no self-mastery; only the life-force of the species. At this depth, the concept of "social" does not even exist.

The contents of the personal and the cultural are acquired (and sometimes *unacquired*) while the contents of the collective element are hardwired, permanent features of human nature. Although the collective element is permanent, it has a limited range of functionality; it is primitive, instinctive, and sometimes aggressive, which pretty much sums up the characteristics of the political animal. The collective element is your alma mater. Translated literally, *alma mater* means "nourishing mother," and this would be true if your mother walked on all fours. Let me state it as plainly as possible: No matter how highly evolved you are, no matter how educated, cultured, well-read, well-traveled, well-paid, or well-known you are, you will always be a lifetime member of this alumni association even if you never pay your dues and never attend reunions.

I have used the word *instinct* (and various derivative forms) several times thus far. Permit me to explain exactly what I mean. *Instinct* refers to thoughts and behaviors that are universally human and present at birth. In other words, your instincts are hardwired, permanent features of your human nature. In micropolitics, instinct consists of three concentric rings: First, instinct functions mentally and emotionally. This includes everything from spiritual and religious instincts, and emotions such as love and compassion, to more organic and physical urges and emotions such as fear and anger. Second, instinct functions as behavior that manifests itself externally and is observable. This includes involuntary bodily functions as well as voluntary actions in relation to (or in response to) your environment. Third, instinct functions socially—with or without the introduction of power to politicize the situation. As stated, these three concentric rings are essential elements of human nature.[9]

If we could peer through a window into human nature, we would find the organization of micropolitics. In its most primitive form, the organization is archetypal, meaning composed of a series of illogical and contradictory images, forms, and patterns. These images are full of meaning—but only if you know the code. (This is why, for example, Ronald Reagan could attract millions of followers but leave others completely baffled or even repulsed.) The pre-logical animal has a strong connection to the collective element, but is incapable of examining its assumptions. Pre-logical human instinct denies self-evident causal connections, disregards the lessons of personal experience, and clings to magical thinking.

Jung compared the collective element to a sea on which your personality sails like a ship.[10] The collective element has many of the qualities of a dream: spontaneous, impartial, unedited, and unfiltered. It exists outside of your will and beyond anyone's control. Given the infinite variations of political differences, and given that people will fight for any reason or for no reason at all, how do you suppose people ever find common ground and come together? Artists, performers, and entertainers who have the greatest commercial success find a way to communicate at this level. They have the ability to express universal symbols and give voice to ideas and images that others only dream about. This is an important characteristic that popular artists share with successful politicians. Recall Ted Kennedy's 1968 eulogy for his brother Robert: Some people dream things that never were and ask, "why not?" The artist's deepest inspiration comes from the collective element, which is the same source as the politician's, even though artists have little or no responsibility for the consequences of public policy.

When Martin Luther King, Jr., dreamt of the day when his children would be judged by the content of their character and not the color of their skin, surely he meant all God's children—all the children of Kenya, Hawaii, and Kansas. When you think about contemporary political leaders, this is why it seems as though you have dreamt about them. Some recent American political leaders, such as George W. Bush, Bill and Hillary Clinton, Sarah Palin, and particularly Barack Obama, seem to be prominent in the dreams (or nightmares) of a great many people—supporters and critics alike. The dreams, images, and myths of the collective are vivid but idealized and generalized, and somehow we are able to see our own reflection when leaders like Reagan or Obama come along.

The cultural element is a thin layer on top of hundreds of generations reaching back thousands of years. In the case of some cultures, such as Germany in the 1930s and '40s, the cultural layer was so thin as to be meaningless, regardless of all the other accomplishments and technological advancements of German civilization. The cultural element may be very clever, articulate, and agile, but it lacks the gravitational force of the collective. In general, the collective element is conservative and reactionary, resistant to change, and more responsive than creative. Once again, I would remind you to follow the advice of Hamilton, Madison, and Jay not to underestimate the dark side of human nature.

In micropolitics, most of the variation is at the personal level. There is less variation at the cultural level and still less at the collective level. I am not suggesting individual characteristics are interchangeable, but more similar than dissimilar. At the collective level, all the unique personalities are reduced to blurry images, archetypes that are recurring examples on one level while being singular examples at another level. More on archetypes later, but think for a moment about the political leaders you admire. In one way, they are all unique personalities, but in another way, each one is a representation of an ideal—a cultural or collective ideal of what a man or woman should be.

There is a herd instinct at the cultural and collective levels. This instinct may be stronger in some cultures and weaker and more susceptible in other cultures. Although politics is an artifact of human nature, different symbols and images will have different meanings, which would be impossible to catalog in this volume. Certain types of events, such as natural disasters, terrorist attacks, or economic depression, may trigger the herd instinct. If the group suffers *as a group* or is somehow victimized *as a group*, then members of the group will respond more or less in unison. When you observe this kind of group behavior, in religious assemblies, sporting events, political rallies, or department meetings—especially the way individual members interact with one another—you can almost see and hear people accessing the same cultural symbols at the same moment.

It is an astonishing thing to observe, for example, when a new university president takes office. There is a ritual (an inauguration) in which the assembled crowd dresses up in robes to pay homage in a tightly scripted ceremony. The ritual usually includes a procession, music and dancing, and speeches of course, followed by a reception (or perhaps a picnic), which is the most important event of the day because this is where people begin jockeying for political position. The costumes, ritual, and elaborate pageantry have a political purpose: to bridge the gap between the cult-hero's ordinary humanity and her new status and position on the totem pole. You may laugh quietly, roll your eyes, or shake your head, but don't dismiss this as one of the peculiarities of academic life. Universities have hundreds (sometimes thousands) of employees, and there are just as many political animals in this kind of organization as in any other. Human nature doesn't change, no matter where you work. Politics is about power, and any situation becomes political the moment power is intruduced.

Please forgive the repetition, but micropolitics is a social affair, and people are not single, separate beings, but members of multiple, overlapping networks, from households to office parks and beyond. As I said in Chapter 2, we have jobs, family ties, and other commitments, which constrain the primitive, instinctive element of our nature and limit our freedom. For the most part, these commitments are voluntary. We transfer our loyalty to a group (family, community, and so on) because we share the same values. This is what Abraham Lincoln meant, in the Gettysburg Address, when he said America was dedicated to a proposition. This dedication to a proposition is a perfect illustration of loyalty based on shared, collective values.[11]

This idea is fundamental to the process of individuation, which we will explore in the next section. As Jung said, "It is obvious that a social group consisting of stunted individuals cannot be a healthy and viable institution; only a society that can preserve its internal cohesion and collective values, while at the same time granting the individual the greatest possible freedom, has any prospect of enduring vitality. *As the individual is not just a single, separate being, but by his very existence presupposes a collective relationship*, it follows that the process of individuation must lead to more intense and broader collective relationships and not to isolation."[12]

In the next section, we are going to continue the inward journey, develop your ability to differentiate between yourself and the cultural and collective elements of your organization, toward the ultimate goal of micropolitics: to become a self-determining agent guided by your own principles instead of the commands and principles of your coworkers without losing your "dedication to the proposition."

Individuation and Consent

In Federalist Paper No. 22 Alexander Hamilton wrote, "The fabric of American empire ought to rest on the solid basis of The

Consent of the People. The streams of national power ought to flow immediately from that pure, original fountain of all legitimate authority." Consent is the only legitimate source of power. Wise rulers—let's call them leaders—cannot rule by force alone and must convince people of their wisdom. And they must persuade people to follow them willingly because of that acknowledged wisdom.[13] I would say the principle of consent is not just the only source of legitimate power, it is also the greatest concept in political science. This principle goes to the foundation of the politician's art and to the heart of your moral authority, which Thomas Jefferson so eloquently described in the Declaration of Independence.

According to political scientist David Beetham, consent is one of the three elements of political legitimacy. Beetham uses the analogy of the tripod. Let's call the first leg *integrity*. Beetham described this as "the acknowledged source of authority underpinning the rules of appointment." This means decision-makers and CEOs should follow established rules, which will minimize nepotism, cronyism, and other forms or corruption. The second leg is the institution's ability to "facilitate achievement." Let's call this leg *skill,* and let's define it in terms of the institution's ability to produce the maximum positive outcome with the least amount of effort and waste. And let's call the third leg consent.[14]

What is consent? Let's begin by explaining what it is not. Consent is not the choice between *willing* or *unwilling* compliance. Consent is not agreement with the range of alternatives imposed on you. With this, I'm talking (again) about the factors that create an unequal distribution of power. When a power structure has jurisdiction over you, it may compel your obedience and force you to behave in a certain way. A court has authority to decide cases within its jurisdiction, for example, just as an executive can make certain decisions within the scope of her jurisdiction. However, the executive's jurisdiction over your body and your behavior—as if you were in a prison or concentration camp—does not extend to your attitude. Your attitude is your choice regardless of any jurisdiction or any organizational power structure to which you belong. One feminist writer said, "Where there is no freedom, there cannot be any consent."[15] This kind of bumper-sticker bravado is hard to argue with. I agree with it, even though it's slightly beside the point, which is that even when you have absolutely no freedom, you always have the power to choose your attitude and give (or refuse to give) your consent.

We can trace the principle of consent back to Thomas Hobbes' *Leviathan* (1651), in which he said the power of free people united by *consent* is the greatest human power. "To have Friends, is Power," Hobbes wrote.[16] I agree with Hobbes (and Madison) that the tendency of people to divide themselves into factions is inherent in human nature. However, to understand politics at this level—the factional level—you have to understand what happens at the elementary level, the interpersonal level, and it has to do with what Hobbes called "masterless men."[17]

Hobbes's 17th-century prose is sometimes hard to follow. Fortunately, political scientist Don Herzog has provided this modern description of the "masterless man": "A familiar figure (not a specter at all) haunts modern society. We've never actually met him, but we all know him. This elusive figure is the free agent, bound only by his own choices. He chooses a career, a spouse, a religion, a lifestyle, and more. He animates our moral and political arguments, our very idea of what a person is."[18] This describes an individual who is by nature free, equal, and independent, and who cannot be subjected to the political power of another without his (or her) consent. The only way she can divest herself of her natural freedom is through her consent.[19] Now, it is important to recognize that Hobbes was writing about the origin of political society in a state of perfect freedom. Nonetheless, Hobbes and Herzog are teaching us one very important lesson about micropolitics: although your natural, unalienable rights (life, liberty, the pursuit of happiness) come from God, your consent comes from you.

These authors are writing about the same type of individual. However, Herzog's term "free agent" is preferable because it is gender neutral, but not as good as the term "autonomous agent." Autonomous agents—men and women—are their own masters, who make their own choices guided by their own moral autonomy. "Autonomy is different from freedom," explained Herzog. "Briefly, an autonomous agent enjoys self-control; he can preserve his ability to make choices; he is not a slave or an addict, and he has self-respect."[20] What is the difference between autonomy and freedom? All the obstacles to autonomy are internal. That is, an external authority may take away your freedom and force you to submit, but can never deny your autonomy or force your consent.

According to the Declaration of Independence, the government's power comes exclusively "from the consent of the governed," not the other way around. This is exactly what gave the American colonies the right to dissolve their political affiliation with the King of England. Their God-given individual freedom and their consent were (and are) two things that no government (and I would add no church and no corporation) can take away. Although the founders never explicitly said the personal is political, nothing could be more personal than voluntarily giving your consent to the government—or giving it to another person.

Clearly, threats of punishment alone are insufficient to guarantee consent, which requires your volition. The "combination of pressures, controls, and repression" said one political scientist, strongly influence your values, beliefs, and moral standards. And more often than not, this obedience follows automatically.[21] But *automatically* does not mean *voluntarily*. This means compliance can be, and often is, merely a habit—a form of conditioned behavior—rather than a conscious choice. If your sense of objectivity is sufficiently elastic and mobile, however, you may remain compliant—on the outside—for any number of reasons: for the sake of appearances, out of loyalty, or because you've calculated the risks of disobedience. Thus, someone may force your submission, compliance, or obedience, but nobody can force you to give your consent.

As we established earlier, the collective is universal, but your personality is unique, which is why the essential political element is the individual. To quote Jung again, "Although biological instinctive processes...contribute to the formation of the personality, individuality is nevertheless essentially different from collective instincts; indeed, it stands in the most direct opposition to them, just as the individual as a personality is always distinct from the collective."[22] I think this is what Aristotle must have meant when he said people are political animals. When you descend deep down to the collective level of the species where humanity is one great anonymous and undifferentiated mass, people are political animals. Your own political individuation begins when you train yourself to hear the primitive voices from past generations.

If self-mastery is important to you, then you have to open a new channel of communication with *the inner friend of your soul*, as Jung called it.[23] This inner friend is your political animal, which, at the end of this process of maturation and transformation, will transcend your personality, keep you from veering toward extremes, and (hopefully) help you refrain from acting on your worst impulses. Remember, politics is about power, and social situations become politicized when power is introduced. You can ignore micropolitics or (try to) avoid it altogether, or you can master this essential social skill for your own self-defense. If mastery is your choice, then you must let your political animal speak. This inner friend is neither your conscience nor the voice of God, but represents your moral authority. If this inner dialog makes you uncomfortable or self-conscious, tell yourself you're only meditating. Whatever your approach, make this truly a two-way exchange. The association will transform you as a result—and you will not be disappointed.

This brings us to the subject of individuation, a two-step process of personal transformation (revolution within) followed by social (specifically political) realignment. Individuation requires imagination and offers the advantage of seeing the space between us all in a different way. As James Hillman said in his masterful book *Re-Visioning Psychology*, "individuation is a perspective."[24] This perspective lifts the so-called *inhumane* aspects of human nature out of the darkness and into the light. As a practitioner, your ongoing self-imposed assignment is to become whole, and this means, if not embracing, at least shaking hands with the animal within. "If every individual had a better relation to the animal within him, he would also set a higher value on human life," said Jung, "Life would be the absolute, the supreme moral principle, and he would react instinctively against any institution or organization that had the power to destroy life on a large scale."[25]

A friendly reminder: politics is about power, not mental health, and individuation is a means to an end: mastering the politician's art. Individuation is not merely desirable but necessary precisely because politics is a social affair. Interacting with people almost guarantees contamination—like any socially transmitted disease. The idea is to guard against political manipulation and emotional contagion by establishing a semi-permeable boundary, which allows legitimate communication but blocks unauthorized access. As I said in Chapter 1, you must be *in* the world (or the office) but not *of* the world. We'll explore this topic in Type 4: the Recluse, but to guard against emotional contagion, you must cultivate the same cool, professional detachment as the medical examiner and not allow yourself to become emotionally involved.

This firewall is necessary because micropolitics is interactive and responsive. When many people share a common emotion, as Jung explained, "the total psyche emerging from the group is below the level of the individual psyche. If it is a very large group, the collective psyche will be more like the psyche of an animal, which is the reason why the ethical attitude of large organizations is always doubtful."[26] Your political self-defense must be proactive because the psychology of large groups inevitably sinks to the level of a mob. For this reason you must journey inward, to where the laws of politics are rooted, in order to equip yourself in your struggle against external authority.[27]

Here, I must pause briefly to acknowledge Raghavan Iyer, one of my favorite professors from college and one of the most remarkable people I have ever known. When I was an undergraduate, I took as many of Iyer's classes as I could, and today salute him for inspiring me to become a political scientist. Iyer's classroom lectures rose to the level of performance art. He would lecture for 90 minutes without notes and after every class receive an ovation from all the students. According to Iyer's obituary, "His...lectures could be spellbinding as he drew from sources from Plato to the Bhagavad-Gita, the Sanskrit poem and classic of Hinduism, from Agatha Christie to the pop songwriter Jackson Browne."[28] Indeed, *spellbinding* is the operative word.

Iyer was born in southern India, educated in Britain, and lived many years in California, and he was fascinated by the process of political individuation. Like many immigrants to America (including my own father), he knew Americans well. He believed that many people—but Americans in particular—functioned from a sense of inadequacy, which led them to seek fulfillment in material things, as if this were possible. This is a variation on Chadwick's Deficit Theory from Chapter 1. If you recall, people feel a deficit (a sense of inadequacy) due to something they believe they have less of than they want or need. This creates an irrational fear that motivates people to overcome the deficit. Fear of not overcoming this deficit is so intense in our modern affluent civilization that it takes all our energy just to keep from falling behind. This competition creates a culture in which many people have no time for looking back or looking forward, no sense of direction, and no tools to take control of their lives. People waste their lives chasing a symbolic sense of achievement, which consolidates their social status among other like-minded people who share the same deficit.[29]

Iyer was not merely a political scientist but also a political visionary. In the politics of the future, he said, credibility would belong not to those who promise material satisfaction (and thus temporary satisfaction), but to those who exemplified authority beyond the limits of any formal power structure and who could speak with urgency and authority about the need for individuation.[30] What is individuation? The shortest definition is "becoming whole," but Carl Jung variously defined individuation as the development of the self, the maturation of personality, and integrating the unconscious into the conscious mind.[31]

Jung also described individuation as the possibility of inner integration and finding the reward in "an undivided self." Individuation is a process of realization. It is a transformation from instinct into spirit, a metamorphosis in which human nature asserts itself up to a point, but then miraculously facilitates the transition from the first half to the second half of your life.[32] In terms of micropolitics, the process of individuation consists of two stages. First, it means finding yourself, reacquainting yourself with parts of your personality you neglected or perhaps never knew about, which necessarily leads to differentiating between yourself and the group. Second, it means realigning yourself socially and reasserting yourself politically. The process of individuation defragments your personality, helps you see beyond yourself, beyond the details of your immediate situation, and mobilizes your power—in terms of personal power (the power *to*) and social power (the power *over*).

Iyer believed the *internalization of authority* was the critical test of individuation. Whether this test is based on logic or faith, said Iyer, "it may be claimed that the achievement of moral autonomy is the mark of moral and spiritual maturity. Instead of being guided by the commands and principles of other people, we must be guided by our own, if we are to be truly self-determining agents."[33] Translation: The more control you assert over the factors within your power, the more of an individual you become, and the more personal your definition of success becomes.[34] This implies there is a strong, positive correlation between the internalization of authority and your mastery of micropolitics.

Does individuation—asserting more control over the factors within your power and living the life of a truly autonomous agent—encourage egocentrism? I would say not. The internalization of authority is somewhat analogous to developing a conscience. The function of the conscience is to form ethical judgments. The conscience is a method of internal condemnation for an act we have carried out—or a wish we have considered. We all have human impulses that exist within us as well as a conscience, a mechanism of inner condemnation that inhibits certain taboo behaviors and/or judges certain taboo behaviors when they are violated. Anything taboo—anything expressly prohibited—conceals a desire, which explains why a taboo is expressed mainly as a prohibition. Obviously, there is no point in prohibiting something nobody desires. Ideally, the process of individuation (personal transformation followed by social realignment) integrates care for oneself with care for others. Individuation, like micropolitics in general, is imaginative and creative, which means the sum of gains and losses can and should be greater than zero.[35] Because individuation is not a zero-sum equation, caring for oneself doesn't preclude caring for others.

As I said in Chapter 1, micropolitics is a working hypothesis that transcends political science and draws from many other fields. As I said in Chapter 2, other social sciences have their place, **but none can supersede the autonomy of the political sphere**. However, this does not prevent us from acknowledging the enormous influence of psychologists, such as Jung and Freud, who challenged—even revolutionized—the way we think about everything. But Freud's influence on all the social sciences, including political science, commands attention and cannot be ignored. Why? It has to do with Freud's pessimism as well as his realism.[36]

Freud's influence as a political scientist began in 1923 with the publication of *The Ego and the Id*. In the first paragraph of this groundbreaking work, Freud divided the mind into the conscious and unconscious, and declared this division to be the fundamental premise of psychoanalysis.[37] This was followed in 1929 with publication of *Civilization and Its Discontents*, which was Freud's most important contribution to political science. Freud observed the fundamental hostility between the individual and modern civilization. He defined civilization as the sum of our accomplishments and technological advancements, all the activities and resources that make life livable, plus all the rules and regulations we impose on ourselves to govern our relations.[38] But civilization is also a process, and in this process we make a bargain. We surrender our freedom in exchange for a little security. We replace the power of the individual with the power of a community.

However, this process of civilization—at least the way Freud described it—is the opposite of individuation and thus runs contrary to the goal of micropolitics, which is to become an autonomous agent guided by your own principles instead of the commands and principles of others. Everyone has an inner self—a political animal that wants to be heard and wants to have an influence on your behavior. But your sense of inadequacy, combined with external pressures and distractions, makes it almost impossible for people to live up to the demands of *the ideal self* without creating irrational fears.[39] Based on this, I think we have discovered an alternative definition of individuation: *living up to the demands of the ideal self.*

Remember though, there are two steps to the process of individuation. Step one is personal: inner integration. Step two is social: political realignment. Both steps are necessary to complete the process. To begin the process, however, I would like you to imagine any "gathering of the faithful," and observe all the people in attendance participating to a lesser or greater extent. If you take a step backward, you'll see not only the members of the congregation and the non-members, but you'll also see the political scientists and other spectators (including me), reading the field.

At this imaginary gathering, you'll see people at one end of the spectrum deeply involved in the ritual, objectively at least. At the other end, you'll see a few people standing near the exit or clustered in groups talking shop, sports, whatever. They are not attentive but neither are they disruptive; they know when to bow and when to kneel at all the right moments. Through careful observation, you may get a sense of the power that the group (or the organization) exerts over members and non-members. The group's fundamental power is the power to confer membership (which may be voluntary or involuntary) and non-membership (which also presumes the power of expulsion).[40] This example reinforces several points applicable to office politics. First, as I said in Chapter 2, the laws of politics are rooted in human nature. Second, these laws are objective and impervious to our preferences. And third, these laws apply to any kind of organization, any family, community, or corporation — anywhere there are two or more people. Instead of a church gathering I might have used a shareholder meeting, a business conference, or a trade show to make a point.

Your fundamental power, which you should never underestimate, is the power to give, or refuse to give, your consent. And as we will see in Archetype 6: The Resister, there is a small universe of difference between submission and consent. Think about this and the process of individuation as we turn our attention to the personal and social implications of self-mastery.

The Meaning of Self-Mastery

In this chapter thus far, we have discussed the collective element, which should have alerted you to the instinctive, primitive, and sometimes aggressive tendencies shared by the entire human species. We have also discussed individuation and the principle of consent, which I believe is the greatest concept in political science. Now I would like to discuss self-mastery, which means becoming the ruler of your inner world, but there's more to it than that. Because micropolitics is a social skill, self-mastery comes partly by gazing at your reflection in the mirror, and also by pushing outward and downward to produce the observable effects of self-mastery.

Self-mastery is important for the same reason the opening break shot in a game of pool is important: If you have no goal in mind and do not care whether you leave the balls in a cluster, touching each other, or touching the rail, then there is no need to master the break shot. Similarly, if you do not care whether you expose your political weakness and announce to all your coworkers—friends and adversaries alike—that *the table is open*, then there is no need to master the principles of micropolitics.

The process of self-mastery proceeds gradually, step by step, which prevents impulsive behavior while simultaneously permitting penetration. Strictly speaking, *penetration* means entering without completely passing through. This precise definition may seem like a trivial semantic distinction, but in terms of self-mastery, penetration indicates a deep and clear perception of a situation. In other words, it indicates objectivity, realism, and thus an accurate reading of the field. This process must develop slowly and deliberately, similar to the formalities of courtship. It is a matter of protocol analogous to the ceremonial etiquette that diplomats follow, or the standard set of rules computers use to communicate with each other across a network. It takes time, which makes unnecessary haste as unproductive as unnecessary leisure.

Why is this? Why must self-mastery proceed like the formalities of courtship, slowly and deliberately? It is because micropolitics is a social skill, which implies the involvement of two or more people. Self-mastery is a necessary step but not the ultimate goal. Nor is the ultimate goal to dominate other people. As stated, the ultimate goal is not the accumulation of power, but the accumulation of virtue, the cultivation of your own character. If you wish to have an enduring, affirmative influence on your environment, your community, your employer, and your family, you must apply the same perseverance—without unnecessary haste or unnecessary leisure—you would require of yourself. You must follow the same careful, gentle, and deliberate course of action.

Some people presume politics is unprincipled, but I believe—precisely because politics involves the use of power—it requires upholding the highest ethical standards. Power corrupts, as Lord Acton said, and there is only one way to respond to this fundamental law, even for masters of micropolitics. And that is by never abusing your power. The principles of micropolitics all point toward this *elementary* principle, which demands that you make the accumulation of virtue a higher priority than the accumulation of power. When you look at your ultimate goal—to grow beyond yourself; to become someone different—from this perspective, you should see something ambitious but also attainable. You should see a goal worthy of your sustained commitment and well within your reach.

What exactly does self-mastery look like? To me, it looks like a multi-dimensional value system with a feedback loop. Social psychologist Milton Rokeach has some insight regarding the value system, which he described as "an enduring organization of beliefs concerning preferable modes of conduct or end-states of existence along a continuum of relative importance."[41] This value system is helpful for understanding self-mastery within the context of micropolitics. First, what is a value? According to Rokeach, a value is your belief about how you ought or ought not to behave, or about a goal that is worth or not worth achieving.[42]

Building on this definition, Rokeach identified "individual" values and "social" values. Individual values are self-centered, whereas social values are group-centered. Then, Rokeach distinguished between "instrumental" and "terminal" values. A terminal value is a goal or preferred end-state. An instrumental value is a code of conduct, a set of rules to guide your responsibilities, decisions, and behavior. He also identified two different types of instrumental values: moral and competence. When you behave consistently with moral values, it means behaving honestly and responsibly, which in turn leads you to feel you are behaving *morally*. When you behave consistently with competence values, it means behaving logically, intelligently, or imaginatively; you are behaving *competently*.

Failure to uphold moral values leads to feelings of guilt, whereas failure to uphold competence values leads to feelings of low self-esteem. Likewise, behaving honestly and responsibly leads you to feel you have morals, whereas behaving logically and intelligently leads you to feel you are competent.[43]

Self-mastery sounds like such a good idea that no one would stand against it. The real trouble with self-mastery is defining it, and setting too low a standard. As an instrument of micropolitics, self-mastery has a personal element and a social element, just as I described in the section on individuation. There are also the systemic elements—moral values and competence values. As a value system, self-mastery does not mean becoming a perfectionist—someone dissatisfied by any behavior *in others* that does not meet your impossibly high standards. Self-mastery means that when you recognize flaws in other people, you are lenient and forgiving. It means that when you recognize flaws in yourself, you are dissatisfied with yourself. In particular, it means channeling your dissatisfaction with yourself to produce the conditions for growth.

The wind blows and the palm tree sways. Your eyes see the visible effect and your mind construes the invisible cause. This metaphor correctly states the task before us. For the vast majority of people, life consists of events and chance happenings that exercise a dominant influence. Self-mastery entails a shift away from responding and toward leading. It implies, simply, that your entire life is governed by your intentions, not by external events. If you asked Betty Friedan—and I believe this applies equally to men and women—she would say it looks very similar to Abraham Maslow's idea of self-actualization. Friedan would say someone who has achieved self-mastery is complete; she has realized her identity and fulfilled her potentialities as a human being.[44]

As you read the field, make sure you are reading and not projecting. Projection takes place when someone unconsciously transfers character traits or emotions to someone else.[45] Most importantly, this projection is unconscious, and ceases to be projection when the projector becomes (or you become) aware of it. We always seem to recognize our political projections afterward. Perhaps it has to do with the highly emotional content, which a skilled psychoanalyst could help us unravel, but that is not our task. Rather, our task is neither to eliminate politics (which is unrealistic) nor to ignore it (which is unsafe), but to master it. Because you cannot outrun your own human nature, this process of reading the field and recognizing familiar patterns entails seeing through your projections, and recognizing them immediately while you are in the moment, not afterward while you deconstruct what you should have said and done.

Self-mastery means being proactive rather than reactive, training yourself to read the political subtext—the story beneath the story—in any situation, whether in the office or in life. Political subtext is information unspoken but implied regarding the thoughts and motives of the players as well as the natural conflict in the situation. Because politics is a social affair, there will always be multiple political subtexts in play depending on the number of participants. You may already be adept at deconstructing political conflict—forensic political science, if you will—and able to understand political subtext after the fact.

As I said in Chapter 1, the physical space of micropolitics is very small, sometimes no more than the space between two dancers. Even so, it is big enough to hold more structures, systems, symbols, instruments, and archetypes than you probably thought possible. That is all well and good, you might say, but what if I'm only halfway through the book and I have an emergency? In that situation, I recommend making political triage your top priority, though you should remember that your duty to take care of other people does not trump your duty to take care of yourself.

When the power differential is not in your favor and your political skills are not fully formed, you should accept the situation and forego pretentious displays. Inward simplicity and economy are critically important sources of strength, which can compensate for meager outward appearances. In general, self-mastery implies cultivating simplicity and economy within yourself and then drawing on these resources when you receive inadequate support from the external environment. Your long-term goal should not be to compensate for negative feedback from the external environment, but to reduce your dependency. Meanwhile, just be persistent. Just keep showing up at the office every day—with a smile—and teach your colleagues a lesson in staying power.

I already mentioned the need to accumulate virtue and cultivate your character. Let me share a story to illustrate the point. In Hermann Hesse's timeless masterpiece *Siddhartha*, the title character is the handsome son of a Brahmin family. He is a loving and dutiful son, the pride of the family, but spoiled, restless, and discontented. One day, when some holy men wander into town, young Siddhartha impulsively decides to join them, to become an ascetic and seek enlightenment through self-denial. When Siddhartha announces his decision, of course his father refuses to give permission. Siddhartha does not back down, nor does he show his father the slightest disrespect. Instead, Siddhartha shows patience, and for the first time reveals a remarkable capacity to think and wait. At last, Siddhartha's father comes to the realization that his son is no longer a boy and decides to let him go.

Thus, Siddhartha joins the ascetics, gives away all his clothes and possessions except for a loincloth and cloak, and begins to wander, meditate, and practice self-denial in search of enlightenment. Eventually, however, young Siddhartha begins to lose interest in this life of emptiness. One day, Siddhartha and the ascetics cross paths with Gautama the Buddha, *the Enlightened One*. This chance encounter convinces Siddhartha the time has come for him to part ways with the ascetics. Siddhartha knows he must choose a new path but somehow also knows he cannot become a monk and follow in the Buddha's path. Instead, Siddhartha thinks for himself and discovers he must reject all teachings and all doctrines, and make his own path.

Obviously, the accumulation of virtue and cultivation of character implies abstaining from flagrant abuses. Likewise, it implies abstaining from petty behavior, selfishness, meanness, and other such misdemeanors. And it means avoiding conflict by preempting that which might create tension or lead to violence. In the workplace, you can do this by moderating your speech and refraining from verbal abuse, unfair criticism, and gossip. By demonstrating this kind of self-mastery—taking care of your own business—you can prevent escalation and keep conflict at a distance. You can distance yourself literally—meaning physically and spatially—but also *temporally*. With self-mastery, time is a resource under your control, which you can use to alter the rhythm and duration of events. The key factor of success is timing. Wait for the turning point, which never comes from brute force but spontaneously from the natural cycle of events. If you act too soon, you will lose the momentum propelling the natural cycle. Recognizing the turning point and waiting for the right moment—despite the bias for action—is in itself an act of self-restraint, and thus self-mastery.

The ability to wait for the right moment has nothing do to with your title, office, or bureaucratic authority but everything to do with mastering the primitive, instinctive elements of your nature. The master of micropolitics has a sense for the invisible.[46] While the CEO, chairperson, and other executives are preoccupied with their positions, their agenda, and their self-image, you watch and wait for exactly the right moment to act. When you learn good timing, you learn to wait for the right moment the way good comedians adjust the tempo of their delivery to make a joke seem funnier than it is. Think of the way Johnny Carson used to peer into the camera with a neutral expression that practically begged for the audience's sympathy. By the time Johnny finally delivered the line, the audience's expectations were so low that anything he said was funny.

As stated, time can and should be a resource under your control. The best evidence of this is the way you manage the gap between environmental stimulus and your response. That is, one measurement of your self-mastery is the time it takes you to recover from shock. Let me use an extreme example to illustrate the point: a terrorist attack. (Any violent attack, natural disaster, or accident would produce the same effect.) Acts of terrorism are ostentatious displays of violence, which are so shocking that most people react emotionally and physically. Emotional symptoms include disbelief, confusion, anger, shame, and fear, and these are just the initial effects. This emotional trauma coalesces into an acute feeling of powerlessness. It is a natural reflex over which we have little control.

Now, I do not want to minimize the psychological shock but emphasize the recovery time, which will decrease as you develop your self-mastery. This is the gap that opens after the shock, but before your response. Your first objective should be to shorten your recovery time. What comes next? Your second objective should be to reacquire your presence of mind, which is a prerequisite to effective crisis management. You must fulfill these two objectives before your response, whatever it is. You must purge your mind of fear and anger, which will otherwise cloud your mind and rob you of objectivity. Until you have reacquired your presence of mind, you should keep still and practice social distancing.

What is social distancing? You have probably heard of crowd psychology or mob psychology (the *mobile vulgus*), meaning the tendency of people in groups to mimic and/or synchronize the behaviors and emotional states of others in the group. People are social animals and their emotions are contagious, especially when primitive emotions—such as fear and anger—find a receptive host. Terror is an emotional trigger with the potential to influence the behavior and emotional state of anyone in the physical or emotional proximity. Through self-mastery, however, you can manage the frequency, proximity, and duration of your social interaction. This requires a little of Siddhartha's presence of mind and his ability to think and wait, all while maintaining an openly respectful expression.

The idea of self-mastery is to combine strength with gentleness, to balance power with humility. It is also important to balance your *external* power with intellectual and emotional strength. Maintaining this balance of internal and external power is useful regardless of your place in the hierarchy. However, the ultimate practitioner of micropolitics maintains this balance of internal and external power and has an influential position. Please take note: I said balance and *an* influential position, not the most powerful office. Think of Mahatma Gandhi, who never held high office, but wielded power through the force of his personality. Now, think of former president Richard Nixon who was very powerful (for a while) because of his high office but obviously crippled inside. The lesson here is to avoid imitating the bad habits of the ex officio type, meaning those false leaders who rely on their bureaucratic authority and their power by virtue of their position.

You've got a political animal living inside you. Perhaps yours is dormant or undeveloped, but if you want to be able to recognize key political moments and act accordingly, eventually you will have to cultivate time (and timing) as a resource. I think most people do not cultivate this resource, or, frankly, even acknowledge it. You will not achieve self-mastery by denying or suppressing your political animal, but by finding the reward, as Jung said, in an undivided self. You are the blacksmith and your tools are the hammer and anvil. You must forge and shape and synthesize the various elements of your nature to make them work together. Your work takes place on the hardened, tempered surface of the anvil that transfers the force of the hammer's blow. This is how you redefine the political mystique and submit yourself to the process of political individuation, which is how an individual becomes differentiated but not disconnected from society.

Political behavior is nothing new, obviously, but micropolitics is certainly new, at least the way I am presenting it here. Micropolitics utilizes no offensive weapons, only defensive tools and techniques. When it comes to micropolitics, there is a line between offensive and defensive techniques, which we must not cross. Why? It is because offensive techniques are effective—and ultimately abusive—due to the corrosive nature of power. The implication is that you must adapt yourself to the demands of the situation, initiating political action only after exhausting all other options. This implies giving your political goals at least the same consideration that you would give to planning a road trip. You would need a car and a road map, as well as a GPS device or perhaps a compass to keep you oriented. You would also have to plan stops for rest and refueling. In other words, you would break down the elements of your journey and consider the logistical details necessary to reach your destination.

Navigating micropolitics requires setting realistic goals but also being circumspect. It requires calculating the power differential between you and your adversary and evaluating the resistance you will almost certainly encounter when others discover your plans. In addition to calculating your adversary's strength, you must gauge your readiness and willingness to persist in the midst of adversity. One of the great advantages of increasing your self-mastery is that it increases your capacity to deal with ambiguity—while not revealing your strength outwardly—as you put your plans into action.

In addition, you should resist the temptation to seek a once-and-for-all solution. You cannot compel people to experience an epiphany or any sudden great awakening. It only happens like that in the movies. The work of self-mastery, like the work of micropolitics, takes place gradually. The effects work their way outward, and will inevitably do so if you are persistent in your program of self-development. If you try to rush this process, you may achieve some superficial success and acquire some ornaments of power and wealth. You will also attract the attention of people who are dazzled by such superficial ornamentation. However, if you withdraw from the world—not a complete recluse but with the same detachment as Siddhartha—you can preempt unintentional provocation and unjustified aggression, and continue the patient work of self-development.

Does self-mastery give you the right *not* to be political? Yes, of course it does. Even if you are a natural leader with extraordinary leadership gifts, it is still a personal choice to lead or not. You have no obligation to engage in worldly affairs. That does not mean sitting on the sidelines lobbing verbal hand grenades—leave that to talk radio hosts. Nor does it release you from mastering the principles. Once you learn them, you have an obligation to keep your house in order even if you never leave the house. Your choice to withdraw from public life need not be permanent. You may reenter at any time because micropolitics will take place whether you like it or not, and whether you master it or not. (For more on this, see Chapter 6, Archetype 4: The Recluse.)

Let me repeat: You must resist the temptation to seek a once-and-for-all solution. You can keep your office adversaries in check temporarily, but that is all. Self-mastery does not require constant action, but it does require constant vigilance and readiness to act depending on the situation. This subtle distinction reveals something very important about micropolitics: You should not assert yourself politically all the time, but you should remain watchful. Let your purpose be to release tension and reduce people's fear and anger. If you are receptive to this teaching, if you take the necessary steps to develop yourself, you will also be able to teach others and empower them. This prospect of constant vigilance with no once-and-for-all solution may seem tiresome, but that is the nature of micropolitics.

Remember the story about the ship's pilot and the gang of mutineers? Once again, let us not permit a good metaphor to get lost in translation: The pilot is you and the gang of mutineers is also you. The pilot represents the personal element and the gang represents the social element, represented by your primitive ancestors who lived thousands of years ago, whose genetic material still lives within you today. One element is the governor and the other is the governed because one is capable of reason while the other is not.

These two elements—the personal and the social—represent the two faces of Janus (the God of thresholds and passages from

Roman mythology). One face looks back toward the primitive world of the cave dwellers, while the other looks toward the future. The backward-looking face does not merely remember the past, but sees across the millennia, and sees each and every event as a chapter in a very old, very long story. The forward-looking face gives you the ability to sense the abstract beginnings of the future, to anticipate change, and assert your jurisdiction. Together, these elements give you the ability to fight and win the revolution within. Does this sound worthwhile? If so, let us acquaint ourselves with the archetypes of micropolitics in Part II.

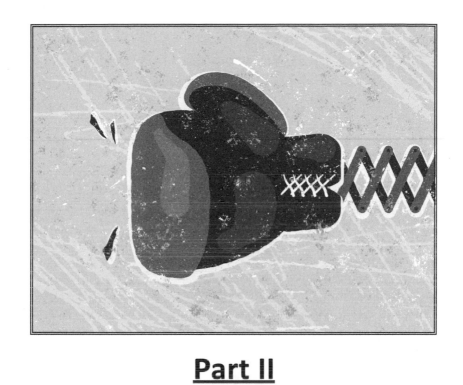

Part II

Defining the Archetypes

Chapter 5

Introduction to Archetypes

Why are archetypes important to office politics? Archetypes are reflections and expressions of your human nature and culture. Archetypes are symbols in concentrated form that communicate what people want, what they fear, and even what they believe is possible.[1] Archetypes are important because symbols are important. Popular artists, musicians, actors—and yes, even successful politicians—are able to tap into symbols and archetypes because they understand intuitively that politics is pre-logical, almost childlike. This characteristic, this ability to manipulate symbols, to assign meaning to practically anything or anyone and thus turn it, him, or her into a symbol, is something that differentiates humans from other species.

A symbol is a shortcut for insiders, which casts a mystique over otherwise ordinary objects and people.[2] Think of Gregory Peck playing Atticus Finch. Think of Ella Fitzgerald and Louis Armstrong singing a Gershwin tune. Think of John Wayne in cowboy hat. Think of Martin Luther King Jr. on the steps of the Lincoln Memorial. Think of Jackie Robinson in a Brooklyn Dodgers uniform. Think of *Green Eggs and Ham*. A symbol projects something intangible and larger than itself, which gives it a dual character, partly real and partly unreal. A symbol may be an object, gesture, relationship, or a linguistic construction, but it stands for something, and produces an emotional and physical response.[3] If a symbol were absolutely and entirely real, there would be no gap into which we could project the symbol's larger meaning, no gap into which we could project political content.

"The archetype is a symbolic formula which always begins to function when there are no conscious ideas present, or when conscious ideas are inhibited for internal or external reasons," said Jung.[4] First, what is a symbolic formula? A symbol is something visible or tangible (such as a flag, a uniform, or a trademark) that represents something abstract. "Symbolic" means *representative*. "Formula" means *prescription*: a set of instructions and a list of ingredients in specific proportion. A symbolic formula is a convenient way to communicate with the environment, send and receive signals (instructions, ingredients, whatever), and classify information. Think of a shortcut on your computer desktop and the way it leads you to a program, file, Website, or external device when you double-click the icon. This is an oversimplification of a fascinating concept and a useful device.[5]

According to the algebraic property of symmetric equality, if an archetype is a symbolic formula, then a symbolic formula is an archetype. One reason we can observe archetypal situations is because all functions and instinctive modes of behavior are similar in humans, the way biological functions are similar among members of the same species. If the basic rationale for evolution is that what worked once will work again, this would explain why people continue to communicate using archetypes and why the shortcut keeps working. If you acknowledge that human nature and human behavior are often instinctive, not necessarily rational, and not completely conscious, then it requires a short leap to see the political archetypes as preexistent forms and patterns of instinctual behavior—in other words, symbolic formulas.

Our exploration into politics, systems, and symbols has naturally led us to Carl Jung, who derived his archetypal approach from his extensive reading of myths, fairy tales, and world literature, but also from his practice as a clinical psychologist in which he analyzed the fantasies, dreams, and deliriums of his patients.[6] Like any dream, archetypes are full of coded meaning. If you ask a psychologist, you might learn that a dream is a secret thought, an unresolved conflict, or a repressed emotion so disagreeable it must be excluded from conscious reflection. Like any dream, an archetype is a façade for a vast edifice that communicates the symbolic formula.[7] However, Jung was a psychologist, not a political scientist.

Whereas a psychologist uses memory material (the specific memories, fantasies, and experiences of an individual) to understand dreams, a political scientist uses a different unit of analysis, which does not come from individual memories, but from something deeper that people share with other people. The archetypes arise out of this element (the collective element from Chapter 4) and thus are not necessarily part of your personal experience. Jung developed the idea of the collective unconscious and differentiated it from the more superficial *personal* unconscious. We have no way of knowing for sure, but it is possible the political archetypes belong to what Jung called the collective unconscious, which he described as the deepest level of the unconscious mind, a kind of subliminal reservoir shared by the entire human species.

Before we proceed, I would like to introduce some vocabulary that will be useful, first to differentiate types of relationships, and second to differentiate the factors that create an unequal distribution of power and which may politicize a relationship. A "symmetrical pair" is a relationship between people who like each other and who influence each other equally—friends and colleagues of equal rank, for example. There is no power differential and there is no politics. An "asymmetrical pair" is a relationship between people whose power and influence is unequal. A supervisor and a subordinate would be the most obvious example. The supervisor has bureaucratic authority and the ability to force the subordinate's submission via threat, intimidation, or coercion. The cause of the inequality may also come from other factors: One person may be more popular, attractive, or charismatic than the other. One may be smarter and better educated or bigger and physically stronger. Finally, one person may dominate the other simply through the force of habit. Any of these factors, or any combination, will create an unequal distribution of power and may politicize the relationship.[8]

Why is the distribution of power in the office important? When the distribution is asymmetrical, a gap opens up. Archetypes fill the gap—the space between us all—with symbolic formulas and patterns of instinctive behavior to compensate for the power differential. When Jung said archetypes begin to function when conscious ideas are inhibited, inadequate, or absent, he implied that individuals are never totally in control. Keeping in mind that Jung is not a political scientist and micropolitics is not therapy, this is good to know given our definition of power *as anything which facilitates control*. This brings us back to our definition of micropolitics, which is an essential social skill whenever people are interdependent and the distribution of power is asymmetrical. What makes a situation *social*? There are at least two people—as in almost any job in any kind of organization. What makes people *interdependent*? Because the organization, whether it is a business, government agency, or academic institution, has a collective goal requiring people to work together. What makes the distribution of power *assymetrical*? Somebody has bureaucratic authority, meaning power by virtue of her position.

Political archetypes, like all symbols, must be sufficiently abstract to resist literal interpretation. They must have an aesthetic value (in terms of sight, touch, sound, color, or texture) that is emotionally appealing and worthy of our attention. Archetypes may or may not reflect the unique experience of any particular individual and/or the local circumstances of any specific culture. They are common to the human race and present in all of us, which partly explains why political conflict takes on familiar, recurring patterns regardless of culture, location, or era. If you work in an organization of any good size, for any duration of time, you might notice how people emulate archetypes and inhabit prepackaged roles, and how the archetypes migrate from one individual to another.

"Archetypal images are among the highest values of the human psyche," according to Jung, and "have peopled the heavens of all races from time immemorial."[9] What does this mean? Why do the archetypes seem to appear and reappear in many different situations involving many different people from many different cultures? Where does the power of political archetypes come from? I have a theory. Have you noticed political leaders who use the plural pronoun "we" when referring to themselves? (This is also known as the *royal we* or the *majestic plural*.) This is not evidence of a split personality or any kind of psychological disorder, but a multiplicity of personal, cultural, and collective forces which effective political leaders use to interact with the environment. The personal element—or persona—is how you symbolize yourself.[10] (There is more on this topic in the following paragraphs.)

It seems unlikely that something as archaic as an archetype could have such potency in our modern office. Given the complexity of politics and the diversity of political behavior across different cultures, I want to assure you this is not science fiction. Still, you may dismiss micropolitics (and perhaps all political science) with the same contempt as you would astrology. You may simply deny archetypes exist because you cannot see them. I cannot see the archetypes, at least not in the conventional sense. I have no proof they even exist. But even without proof, and even if the smartest people in the world convinced us that archetypes could not exist, we would have to invent them, wrote Jung, "to keep our highest and most important values from disappearing."[11] However, I do not think anyone invented the archetypes. What could possibly be the purpose? A far more likely scenario is that the archetypes emerge spontaneously the same way a catalytic reaction takes place.

Although I believe the political archetypes have existed as long as human society, you have a right to be skeptical even if you recognize some or all of the archetypes from your personal experience. You may have inhabited one or two, or you may recognize them in a friend, colleague, or your boss. You may even have fantasized about them. However, the power of the political archetypes should be evident to anyone who has studied history. (Likewise, these archetypes will be less meaningful to those with limited knowledge of geography, history, and literature, not to mention politics.) If some of the archetypes seem familiar to you, this is because micropolitics expresses itself (and people express themselves) through archetypal behaviors. I would hope you recognize this and feel a familiarity, even if you do not entirely understand it all when you are in the middle of events as they unfold.

Although the political archetypes have attributes that defy rational interpretation, we know where they live. Political archetypes require an environment (a gap) that satisfies a specific set of criteria (an unequal distribution of power), which sets them apart from Jung's psychological archetypes. Jung's archetypes all originated on the inside because it would be inconceivable that psychological archetypes could originate *anywhere* in the outside world. Political archetypes, on the other hand, live in the space between us and feed on social intercourse, giving cues, taking cues, and being responsive. This *mutual interpenetration* is an essential element of politics.[12] The only thing missing, the only thing necessary to bring the archetypes to life, is for someone to introduce power into a social situation. This is why politics is so dynamic, because we are not just dealing with individuals, but also with social forces (cultural and collective forces) charged with immense power.

The Political Persona

Before we proceed to the next chapter, which describes the eight political archetypes, I would like to make an important point about recognizing patterns, and reading and playing the field. The archetypes may seem too abstract to be practical in your office situation, at least as I have explained them thus far. As I said earlier, an archetype is a symbolic formula and vice versa, and a formula is a set of instructions and list of ingredients. This may still be too abstract, but keep it in mind. Think of an archetype as a parade of the personal, cultural, and collective elements marching together across the millennia.[13] The personal element is the high-stepping drum major, carrying a baton and keeping the beat. Right behind her is the cultural element—the marching band all in uniform with plenty of brass and percussion. Behind them is the collective element—gigantic animal-shaped balloons and beautifully decorated floats.

As stated, archetypes are not of your own making but the result of a multiplicity of systemic forces. The collective element is a depository of thousands of years of human experience, separate from you but still connected to you. The cultural element socializes and conditions you, but also signals membership/belonging to a family, organization, community, or other kind of group. Working together, the cultural and collective elements maximize your cultural affiliation and common humanity. The personal element—or persona—is the symbol-carrier, which puts a human face on the cultural and collective elements.

Your persona is not how you actually are, but how you appear to yourself or to the world. According to Jung, "The persona is a complicated system of relations between the individual consciousness and society, fittingly enough a kind of mask, designed on the one hand to make a definite impression upon others, and, on the other, to conceal the true nature of the individual."[14] Translation: Your persona is the camouflage you wear, which you have developed based on observing the effect you have on the world. In micropolitics, the persona is a social façade you use purposely to conceal your motives and interests. It's your poker face. In the workplace, you should wear your poker face in any important negotiation, any working committee, or any other formal meeting. This is what it means to be in the thick of it! As stated, a good poker face is a façade that allows you to think things through and make up your mind *in private* even when you're in the public eye.

No effective politician presents her true self to her adversaries, her allies, or even her friends.[15] Effective politicians wear a mask. I would not say *all the world's a stage and we are merely players*, but I would say success in politics is impossible without the ability to present a simple, even caricatured version of your true self. Furthermore, don't flatter yourself by disparaging the hypocrisy of it all. Why? This is another intersection in which power and leadership converge. If you are leading *without* exercising power, it is an absolute necessity to maintain the continuing stream of interaction, to ensure the circle of cue-giving and cue-taking remains unbroken.

In micropolitics, there is an additional advantage of an alternate persona, which has to do with your emotional well-being. Remember, politics is a social activity that requires the participation—active or passive, voluntary or involuntary—of at least one other person. This means getting up close and personal, interacting, responding, attracting criticism, or inviting attack. If people in your organization are harassing or bullying you, remember they are harassing and bullying your persona, the false self you have purposely developed to conceal your motives and interests—or, in this specific context, to shield yourself and your emotional well-being. If people criticize or attack your persona, you can sit back and laugh because the attacks and criticism are directed not at you, but at your creation, your fictitious political persona. It is impossible to overstate the advantage of this.

For the purposes of micropolitics, your "tactical self" is a façade whose purpose is to protect you and your emotional well-being, and to control your emotions in order to free your mind for more urgent problems.[16] Even if you are facing insults and verbal abuse in the office, your situational awareness should remain unaffected because your tactical self is keeping you in the moment and in control. If you lose your temper, you lose the game. If you show emotion—especially if you have been provoked—you lose the ability to think and act rationally.

The tactical self is also useful for gathering intelligence. A case in point: If you want to learn more about the political forces opposing you in your organization, try disrupting the bureaucracy on some minor detail. If you need an official signature, for example, approach the signatory directly rather than sending the document through normal channels. Even if your behavior was entirely intentional you can act as though it was a simple misstep and then act as if you were contrite. It is imperative, however, that your *mark* never discovers your true goal. Even so, this kind of manipulative behavior creates a byproduct. You may think you are getting away with something, that you will be immune from the corrosive effects of power, but remember that nobody can outrun her own human nature.

Although micropolitics requires a public face and a private face, the faces (façades) cannot be so dissimilar as to be completely different people. These days, you cannot rely on fooling people for an entire 24-hour news cycle, let alone all the time. In a way, you must *be* exactly whom you pretend to be, but you still have to pretend. The idea is to be as disciplined in your private life as you are in public, and if you cannot, then you have to adjust one side or the other, or both. I am not just talking about the obvious cases such as the sexually promiscuous (or abusive) religious leaders. I am talking about vertical consistency at every level.

Let me repeat: The purpose of micropolitics is to teach political self-defense, not how to run con games or play dirty tricks on co-workers. The way you use your power and conserve your resources is at the root of self-mastery. Learning to use your tactical self as a defensive shield to protect your emotional well-being is evidence of self-mastery, maturity, and the ability to impose and enforce limitations on yourself. Limitations may be annoying but they are indispensable in micropolitics because they help you avoid extremism. By setting effective limitations, you channel your resources toward your goals. The idea of unlimited possibilities may seem attractive, but unless you eliminate peripheral distractions you risk letting your goals dissolve into nothingness.

The personal element of self-mastery is synonymous with self-restraint but not to the extent that it runs contrary to human nature. So, as you work toward self-mastery, keep realistic expectations about yourself and others, and remember that excessive limitation is an invitation to rebellion. Individuals attain significance, in my opinion, only by surrounding themselves with limitations and determining for themselves what their duty is. The material world is transitory, and nothing in it is more transitory than politics. But there is nothing more sublime than devotion to duty, even in our networked, high-tech world. If you are willing to pay more attention to duty than the ordinary person, then I would like to introduce you to some old friends of mine: *The Gods of Micropolitics.*

Chapter 6

The Gods of Micropolitics

Legendary political scientist Harold Lasswell wondered whether there exists a basic political type, an *anthropo politicus* or political human.[1] I think we have answered that in the affirmative, but let me repeat what I said at the beginning of the book: At certain times, certain people will devalue other things in their lives (wealth, health, respect, morality, or love) relative to the acquisition of power. At certain times, certain people will calculate that political behavior will serve this interest more than other types of behavior.[2] However, merely wanting power is not enough, because there are variables that must be considered in the political calculus. These are:

1. The degree to which the situation lends itself to personal intervention.

2. Your position and status.

3. The strengths and weaknesses of all individuals in the situation.

To repeat, if the situation is unstable such that the actions of a single individual could affect the outcome, then the variable of skill becomes very important because the greater your skill, the less dependent you are on the situation being favorable, the less dependent you are on being strategically placed within the situation, and the greater the likelihood your skill (rather than someone else's) will determine the outcome.

This brings us back to Lasswell's question: Is there a basic political type? Yes, but there are other types as well, not necessarily "basic" but equally interesting. There are those who have power without wanting it, and those who want it without having it. Then there are those who have power and want it—and they want it so badly they cling to it until their last breath. One characteristic all power-seekers share is their "intense and ungratified craving for deference."[3] People who fit the basic type tend to project themselves into social space (outward and downward) and take possession of people and things beyond themselves and far beyond the basic orientation of the extroverted type. In some cases, this compels them to enlarge their personal boundaries and transform family members, friends, their job, subordinates, and even coworkers into items of personal property.

As I have mentioned throughout the book, the politician's art requires social intercourse: giving cues, taking cues, and being responsive. In this context, the myth of the self-made, self-contained man (or woman) is grossly misleading. And before we turn to the archetypes, I want to say a few words about leadership, and especially about the similarities and subtle differences between power and leadership. Leadership always depends on the response of followers, on the cue-taking circle remaining unbroken.[4] Leadership isn't something that an individual has all the time in every situation. If people respond, there is leadership. If people don't respond favorably and voluntarily—if they don't take the cue—there is no leadership. No exceptions.[5]

I want to be sure you've got the meaning of leadership without undo interference from me. Let's read political scientist Andrew McFarland's definition as well as his reasoning. "A *leader* may be defined as one who has unusual *influence*." So far so good, but power is not the same thing as influence. What is influence? How is it different from power? McFarland offers this helpful definition: Influence is one's capacity to make people behave differently than they otherwise would. This definition is helpful because it does not encroach on our definition of power. What is power? Power is anything that facilitates *control* of one human over another. So, what is the difference between influence and power? The difference is control. With leadership, you can (using a variety of techniques) cause people to behave differently, but with power you can *force* people to behave differently.

Let's continue to follow McFarland's line of reasoning. "A leader may also be defined as one who has unusual power. Here we view 'power' as a person's capacity to make others do something that they would not do otherwise."[6] Reading this, it may seem as though McFarland does encroach on our definition, but no. Why? Leaders *may* be powerful, they *may* exercise power, but not necessarily so. There may be an overlap, and there often is, but not necessarily. Let's use an extreme example to illustrate the point. On November 22, 1963, Lee Harvey Oswald assassinated President John Kennedy. On this day, Oswald exercised great influence on the course of human events. You could argue that Oswald was not merely influential, but more powerful than the average legislator. Does this constitute leadership?

Obviously not, but let's test it anyway. Oswald exercised great influence, and for a moment, great power. This was an example of an extremely lopsided power relationship, in which one party lost everything.[7] Oswald exercised power the same way a mugger who shoots you dead and steals your wallet exercises power. The mugger does not give you a choice, and this makes the "power exchange" not just unfair but also involuntary. Let's alter the scenario slightly: the mugger demands your wallet first and then threatens to shoot if you don't hand it over. In this scenario, the mugger has issued a threat in order to alter your behavior. This exchange exemplifies how a situation becomes politicized when power is introduced. But leadership doesn't depend on power. It depends on the voluntary response of the followers. Thus, there is no leadership in this power exchange.

As stated, leadership is a specific social or interpersonal situation in which someone responds favorably and voluntarily to a leadership cue. Leadership is always defined by a specific situation and realized in the response of followers. If followers respond favorably and voluntarily, there is leadership. If followers do not respond favorably and voluntarily, there is no leadership. Part of leading people—whether in life or in the office—means knowing when to use power and when not to use it.[8] Knowing when *not* to use power will help you *not* politicize a relationship. This can be very difficult if you are already powerful and you regularly receive empowering responses from people around you.[9] This is challenging when you consider leadership as a form of conditioning, which depends on the cue-giving/cue-taking circle (the exchange) remaining unbroken.

The confusion between politics and leadership is understandable because both require social interaction. In certain political relationships, there is an expectation that a negative response (failure to complete the circle) comes with a sanction (a punishment): *Do as I say or you're fired.* This is condign power, which seeks to alter someone's behavior via threat, intimidation, or coercion. In other political relationships, there is an expectation that a positive response (again, success in completing the circle) will come with a reward: *If you do as I ask, you'll be promoted.* This is compensatory power, which seeks to alter someone's behavior by offering money, gifts, recognition, jobs, promotions, and such. As I said in Chapter 4, consent implies permission, affirmation, acceptance, and willingness, all of which are indeed responses that complete the circle. However, producing this kind of learned response using the threat of punishment or the promise of reward does not qualify as leadership, which must be ratified by the support (the consent) of the followers.

Leadership requires knowledge and know-how—knowing the principles of micropolitics, for example, and knowing how to apply them to tap into resources and attract a political following.[10] Maintaining the leadership circle—the circle of cue-giving and cue-taking—is a question of creating confidence, first by creating an expectation that you will do what you say, and then by doing it. Creating and fulfilling expectations reinforces your legitimacy, and increases the faith and trust people feel toward you. But most importantly, creating and fulfilling expectations helps ensure the circle of cue-giving and cue-taking remains unbroken. In the workplace, it would be less risky never to make promises. This would certainly mean less disappointment and dissatisfaction. However, this would also mean less opportunity for leadership. So, make promises. Make them and keep them. If you say you're going to do something, do it, and cross it off your list. This is how you increase the faith and trust people feel toward you. And it is perhaps the best, most cost-effective leadership habit you can acquire.

It is easy to see how the expectation works in two situations. That is, it is easy to see the follower's incentive to complete the circle when the leader holds the carrot or the stick. What about conditioned power? It is harder to see how sanctioned expectation would work in this situation.[11] If leadership is *always* defined by a specific situation and always recognized in the response of followers, then how do you lead when it is so easy for leaders and followers alike to break the circle? Remember, conditioned power implies the ability to alter someone's behavior through persuasion and education—no carrot, no stick, no reward, and no punishment; just leading by example and modeling behavior you hope others will emulate. This is what I meant at the end of Chapter 5 when I said self-mastery is synonymous with self-restraint. When you make a conscious choice to rely exclusively on conditioned power, you impose limitations on yourself.

My purpose here is to highlight the interactive and responsive elements of micropolitics. When I say political archetypes require an environment that satisfies a specific set of criteria, and that we know where the archetypes live, I mean the intersection of cue-giving and cue-taking. This is the intersection where power and leadership converge. I am not suggesting power and leadership are synonymous because the sanctioned expectation in a political relationship is unique. Nonetheless, the continuing stream of interaction—cue-giving and cue-taking—is an absolute necessity no matter which instrument of power you use, and no matter whether you use power at all. The necessity of getting up close and personal—of interacting and responding—is also precisely what makes it a challenge to recognize patterns and read the field. One practical advantage of the archetypal approach, however, is that it lets you step back a little to see the patterns and recognize which archetype is dominant in a situation.

In Chinese folklore, the Eight Immortals are popular mythological figures that symbolize prosperity, longevity, healthy children, and good reputation. The Eight Immortals are depicted in numerous paintings, sculptures, and tapestries, and, according to legend, they are known as scholars, genies, fairies, or philosophers with the power to give life, help people in distress, and punish wrongdoers. And so it is with political archetypes. For the sake of tradition, I have also limited the number here to eight. Why eight? I'll let James Hillman respond: "Leadership entails learning the patterns, learning the ways of the Gods, so that one does not fall prey to the monotheistic simplification of *one size fits all*."[12] Although there are eight distinct types, it would be impossible to tear one away from the others and examine it in isolation. Each one is a subsystem belonging to a more complex system, or, if you prefer, a tool in the toolbox. Here is a brief summary of the eight political archetypes, the constituent elements of *anthropo politicus*:

1. **The Servant-Leader:** This archetype leads by example and wins the consent of her followers without resorting to threats of punishment or promises of reward.

2. **The Rebel:** This archetype personifies the opposition leader, living proof that a certain amount of political conflict is inevitable.

3. **The Mentor:** This archetype is the counselor who facilitates, mediates, and negotiates, and thus acquires great influence over important decisions.

4. **The Recluse:** This archetype personifies professional detachment, and refuses (or appears to refuse) to participate in political gamesmanship.

5. **The Judo Master:** This archetype personifies the Archimedean principle of leverage and using your adversary's power to win without fighting.

6. **The Resister:** This archetype personifies the individual who may be overpowered, but continues to follow her political conscience and refuses to give her allegiance.

7. **The Opportunist:** The archetype personifies tactical dislocation: distracting your adversaries, disrupting their plans, and exploiting their most vulnerable point.

8. **The Survivor:** This archetype personifies the individual who has lost everything but never surrenders her moral authority.

As stated, micropolitics is a combination of one-time calculation and general pattern recognition—and for the rest of this chapter the emphasis will now shift to pattern recognition. As you read each section in the rest of this chapter, consider the similarities and subtle differences between power and leadership. Notice that some archetypes are always proactive (No. 1, the Servant-Leader, for example) while others take the initiative only in response (No. 5, the Judo Master, for example). By mastering all of the archetypes instead of relying habitually on one or two, you can win people over not just by threats of punishment and promises of reward. If you truly want to lead people—and there is no field where this is truer than in office politics—now you have an ethical alternative.

Type 1: The Servant-Leader

One of my favorite scenes in David Lean's epic movie *Lawrence of Arabia* takes place between T.E. Lawrence (played by Peter O'Toole) and the great Bedouin warrior Auda abu Tayi (played by Anthony Quinn). Lawrence and Auda are sitting in Auda's tent after a good meal. In the dramatized scene, Lawrence is trying to convince Auda to join the Arab Revolt. Lawrence questions whether Auda is merely a "servant" of the Turks, who control the vital seaport at Aqaba. Lawrence's question is more of a taunt than an insult, but Auda cannot resist taking the bait:

"I carry twenty-three great wounds, all got in battle. Seventy-five men have I killed with my own hands in battle. I scatter, I burn my enemy's tents. I take away their flocks and herds. The Turks pay me a golden treasure. Yet, I am poor, because I am a river to my people! Is that service?"[13]

Well, is that service? How shall we answer Auda's question? It depends on your values: If leadership is more important to you than accumulating personal wealth, then Auda is the archetypal Servant-Leader. By way of comparison, here is Raghavan Iyer's expressive description of the Servant-Leader: "He must identify himself with the dreams, activities and sufferings of the people. His life must be a continual sacrifice of self in the immediate service of his fellow men. He must be a monk, striving to be a saint, willing to be a martyr, a non-violent revolutionary, a moral educator who can bring about a new political consciousness and creative social awareness among the masses."[14] Clearly, Iyer had Mahatma Gandhi in mind when he was writing this because he also said such a leader should never occupy any formal office or position of power. It is true Gandhi never held high office, but this does not make servant-leadership and bureaucratic authority in the office mutually exclusive.

Gandhi was as fascinated by power as any political scientist, and as ambivalent about it as any psychologist. This, said Iyer, was because Gandhi consistently looked at politics from the perspective of the rebel rather than the ruler (more on the Rebel archetype in the next section). Given Gandhi's charisma, communication skills, and moral authority, any formal office or position of power would have been superfluous. However, Gandhi was skeptical about office-holders in any bureaucracy, and the reason (I believe) is because he understood human nature all too well, and knew enough about his own weaknesses and failings to make him uncomfortable with the idea that people would shape their conduct based entirely on *his* words and actions.

As stated, politics is an exchange between someone who wants power and someone (or a group) who wants to confer that power on someone else. Leadership requires a different kind of response, a different kind of consent beyond the limits of any relationship based on domination and submission. For this reason, the Servant-Leader archetype entails not merely nurturing yourself but also nurturing the people around you. Remember, there is very little leadership potential emanating from anyone's place on the organizational chart, which requires servant-leaders to fill the gap between their job description and their human potential. Now, it is certainly possible to produce a learned response using threats of punishment and promises of reward. But these instruments of power may even hinder your ability to lead, which means you should probably exclude power from your definition of leadership.[15]

Let me give you an example. In 1963, a few days after John Kennedy was assassinated and Lyndon Johnson became president, Johnson gave a speech to Congress in which he urged Congress to pass a civil rights law and eliminate race-based discrimination, saying there could be no better way to honor Kennedy's memory. "We have talked long enough in this country about equal rights," he said. "We have talked for one hundred years or more. It is time now to write the next chapter, and to write it in the books of law."[16] As the ultimate authority figure—President of the United States—it was still difficult for Johnson to lead the fight for civil rights. Leading the fight, creating a sense of urgency, and generating political will was the job for Martin Luther King Jr. and Roy Wilkins (then executive secretary of the NAACP) while Johnson worked the telephones, lobbied legislators, and assembled a winning coalition.[17] The result was the landmark Civil Rights Act of 1964. The point, again, is that leadership isn't something that any individual (even the president) has in every situation. Leadership doesn't emanate from your place on the organizational chart, and it may even prevent you from leading. To lead is to create a following. If no one is following, you're not leading.

In our celebrity-obsessed popular culture, the idea of moral authority may seem like a quaint artifact, but servant-leaders must learn to appeal to the *better angels of our nature* because no one—not even skeptics, cynics, or political scientists—can shake themselves free of their own human nature. Remember, the laws of politics are impervious to our preferences. Remember also that politics has its own peculiar logic, its own standards, and its own ways of measuring success. Servant-leadership does not require you to sacrifice your job or your freedom to achieve your goals. On the contrary, mastering micropolitics is the surest way to avoid becoming a martyr. The Servant-Leader and the martyr may share the same goals, and may even use similar tactics, but the Servant-Leader does not have to die to succeed, whereas the martyr cannot separate suffering and death from success.

When I say *moral authority* I want to be precise because the Servant-Leader archetype implies developing greatness of spirit forceful enough that people think twice before initiating or escalating conflict. Jung comes close in this poetic description: "In keeping with its original wind-nature, spirit is always an active, winged, swift-moving being as well as that which vivifies, stimulates, incites, fires, and inspires."[18] Moral authority precedes authentic leadership. The idea is not external ornamentation, but spiritual development, which is necessarily internal, invisible, and inscrutable to others.

Moral authority works outward from within, which means, among other things, your verbal communication must be consistent with your conduct and other aspects of your professional life. If there is nothing behind your words, they will have no meaning and you will have no influence beyond threats of punishment and promises of reward. Your words acquire weight when they influence your conduct, and subsequently influence the conduct of other people as well. In addition, your conduct should be consistent over time. This does not mean you must adhere to a rigid orthodoxy and not learn anything new; it means your outlook should become more future-oriented even as you hold to traditional beliefs and customs. In a nutshell, authentic leadership means increasing your far-sightedness and decreasing your need for instant gratification.

If you are a servant-leader—or any kind of leader, good or bad, in or out of the office—it implies seeing and being seen. If you enjoy a commanding view, then you are also visible from afar; a familiar sight on the cultural landscape. Have you carefully considered the responsibilities that go along with this? First, the way you live your life is as important as anything you say, but this does not mean you have to be a monk. Second, your verbal skills may help you become well-known in our media-driven culture, but unless you cultivate your inner life, little of what you say will produce lasting results.

Politics is interactive and responsive, but the response is not guaranteed, which is why cultivating your leadership skills and cultivating your inner life must go hand in hand. This cultivation and spiritual development is another form of conditioning.

But I digress. Micropolitics is still about power. Micropolitics remains a social skill. Emulating the Servant-Leader archetype means minimizing other things that you value for the sake of power, which is a point I have made several times. The one thing you may not (must not, should not) do is forfeit, minimize, or compromise your self-mastery. Jigoro Kano, the founder of modern judo, shared this homespun insight about the relationship between servant-leadership and self-mastery: If you want to do something to help society, he said, first you've got to take care of your own business.[19] Although Kano was writing about judo and the many benefits of martial arts training, he was also expressing timeless truths that no Samurai (or Bedouin warrior for that matter) could fail to appreciate. *Samurai* literally means "one who serves," and who serves according to a code that emphasizes all the noble characteristics and conduct of a medieval knight, such as valor, honor, courtesy, generosity, and loyalty.

Well, is this service? Is this leadership? Let's allow Raghavan Iyer to respond. "The true leader," according to Iyer, "shows his capacity to assume heavy burdens of responsibility by taking upon himself the errors and failings of those weaker than he is."[20] Once again, Iyer was referring to Gandhi, who was a kind of archetype of an archetype. The point for this archetype is that you must be with your people, stay in touch with them, and share their ups and downs. A leader is the first link in the chain, but the chain is only as strong as the weakest link. If you only look upward—only for people who can promote you—but never look outward or downward, you will break the cue-giving/cue-taking circle essential to leadership. In the vocabulary of management, this means flattening the hierarchical structure, eliminating barriers between you and your colleagues, your clients, and anyone you want to lead.

If the "true" leader assumes the burdens of responsibility and takes upon herself the errors and failings of those weaker than herself, then how would you describe the false leader? In a corporate environment, they are easy to recognize. They take credit for the most trivial successes but seldom take responsibility when things go wrong. They blame the results of their own shortsightedness on the stagnant economy, their predecessor, their competition, or some other convenient factor, but never on their own flawed strategy. False leaders are weak, insecure, and unable to overcome their own fears of disloyalty and secret resistance. Most importantly, they rely a little more than they should on the threat of punishment and the promise of reward.

Psychologist Abraham Kaplan offered an interesting way to differentiate between authentic and false leadership. Kaplan's approach requires observing the "structure of responsibility," running parallel to the bureaucratic structure. An authentic leader isn't a puppet who mouths the words of a ventriloquist. An authentic leader isn't a spokesperson who repeats official policy. An authentic leader takes responsibility before and after—long after—she makes a decision, while the false leader does not. An authentic leader assumes she must live with the consequences of her decision, while a false leader epitomizes the IBG-YBG mentality—"I'll be gone and you'll be gone"—and presumes they will be out of office or out of town before the bill comes due.[21]

The false leader will never attain what political scientist Aaron Wildavsky called the highest stage of leadership. This phrase comes from Wildavsky's book *The Nursing Father: Moses as a Political Leader*, in which Wildavsky describes Moses as "a leader who taught his people to do without him by learning how to lead themselves."[22] I agree with Wildavsky's assessment about Moses, but teaching people do to without you so they can lead themselves isn't the highest stage of leadership. It's the lowest, most essential, and thus most indispensable. If you aren't teaching people do to without you,

you aren't leading. "The good leader uses force when necessary," wrote Wildavsky, while "the great leader seeks to make force unnecessary."[23] I can say with confidence that Raghavan Iyer would agree with this observation (the difference between good leadership and great leadership), especially when you consider Gandhi's long struggle to make force unnecessary. This is an example of leadership without power, or, more specifically, leading (teaching, conditioning) without threats of punishment and promises of reward.

George Orwell's masterpiece *Animal Farm* is loaded with symbols and archetypes that show how intoxicating power is, and how susceptible people are to conceit, envy, greed, hypocrisy, pride, and vanity. To refresh your memory, *Animal Farm* begins when farmer Jones of Manor Farm goes to bed and all the animals on his farm gather to hear his prize pig, called "Old Major," give a speech. Old Major is a prophet who foretells a future in which animals, not humans, will run the farm some day and enjoy the fruits of their own labor. One day, farmer Jones gets drunk and forgets to feed the animals, which provokes the animals into rebellion. The animals take over the farm and rechristen it "Animal Farm."

The pigs become the organizers and the leaders of Animal Farm. Two of the cleverest ones, Snowball and Napoleon, turn Old Major's prophecy into an ideology called Animalism, complete with commandments, such as *all animals are equal.* Snowball is a natural leader, a visionary, and an expert administrator. Napoleon is the master tactician. Predictably, the unity following the rebellion disintegrates, and Snowball and Napoleon argue frequently. While Snowball keeps busy managing the farm, Napoleon declares that educating the young is of utmost importance and assumes guardianship for two litters of puppies recently born on the farm. The little puppies grow into big dogs and become Napoleon's body guards. When one of the frequent disagreements between Snowball and Napoleon comes to a head, Napoleon sets the dogs on Snowball and chase him away from the farm. Thus, the rebellion becomes a coup d'état. Napoleon moves out of the pigsty and into the farmhouse where farmer Jones previously lived, breaks one commandment after another, and things really begin to unravel.[24]

In almost any family or any organization, you will encounter false leaders who are highly self-conscious of their title. They display this self-consciousness (and psychological insecurity) by the way they categorize everyone relative to their own position in the hierarchy. This misguided over-emphasis on obedience and conformity would be harmless except such "leaders" expect you to share their bureaucratic and legalistic mentality because it feeds their hunger for recognition. The thing they want from you may seem inconsequential, but the instinctive drive for recognition in human nature is almost impossible to overstate. You can afford to give recognition in small doses to the false leader, but give too much and you risk turning a clever little pig into a monster.

The self-perception of false leaders, particularly those at the top of the hierarchy, tends to exacerbate all those unflattering human vices the founding fathers listed. When there is nobody in the hierarchy above you, no matter how large or small the hierarchy may be, it plays tricks on your mind and distorts your judgment (see No. 5 in First Principles). If you are always restless and dissatisfied, you will be tempted to advance for the sake of the reward rather than for the sake of meaningful accomplishment. For those who habitually spend their careers climbing the ladder and accumulating titles, servant-leadership will not come naturally. It's not impossible, it's just harder for some than for others to discard ornamentation and lead by example. This idea, like the idea of moral authority, may seem like another quaint artifact, but you should resist endlessly storing up treasures on earth—especially the kind attractive to moths and thieves. The servant-leader is content with simplicity, concentrates on serving others, and does not waste her talents and energy on unworthy people and things.

When you assert your leadership and people respond favorably and voluntarily, you will attract a following. After all, ask yourself how you know when someone is a leader. A leader has followers who share her beliefs and help spread her message. This is the most benign form of mutual interpenetration, which is an essential element of the politician's art. But what else does it mean to be a follower? For those who are intellectually lazy, it means never having to take responsibility except as self-appointed guardian of the leader's image. This is not how followers see themselves because they consider it their solemn duty to keep tabs on the faithful, convert skeptics, and denounce non-believers, all with a little more zeal than the original archetype. The worst are the sycophants who feed on psychological insecurity, insinuate themselves into the inner circle, and increase their influence through flattery. The word *sycophant* comes from Greek, and describes an overly obedient and deferential individual whose behavior is servile, submissive, *and ultimately self-serving*. Would you want to be surrounded by people who fawn over and flatter you? Would you want to become one? No one respects them and no one should trust them, least of all the objects of their deference. The Servant-Leader must avoid surrounding herself with toadies and sycophants who enable false leadership.

Psychological insecurity is particularly detrimental to an organization because it requires so much energy to compensate for it, and because it diverts time and energy inward (toward employees) instead of outward (toward the organization's mission). If you've spent time in almost any kind of organization you are familiar with the problem of office-holders who can't stand to have anyone around them who could do a better job running the organization, and who surround themselves with toadies, sycophants, and incompetents. The more psychologically insecure the office-holder, the greater the need will be to centralize authority and control (or try to control) the organization. False leaders, crippled by their psychological insecurity, can destroy an organization and damage the lives of the people who work there.[25]

I do not want to suggest that attracting a following is a negative experience but briefly call attention to the downside. If the Servant-Leader archetype were a dance, it would certainly not be freestyle. It would look more like the tango: a posture and an attitude; elaborate footwork and complex movement, a leader and a follower joined in a fluid embrace.[26] The give-and-take of micropolitics can inspire works that would be impossible except as the collaborative effort of many dedicated and talented people. This, in the words of Albert Camus, is "the profound joy experienced by the man of action in contact with a large section of humanity."[27]

Nonetheless, the Servant-Leader requires exceptional self-restraint. Even if you refrain from threats of punishment and promises of reward, power is corrosive. As Carl Jung said, "the superstitious belief in verbal statements" is one of the greatest failures of our civilization.[28] When I first read this, I thought Jung was referring to the superstitious (and uneducated) masses who believe things despite evidence to the contrary. But now I see he was talking about the lies we tell ourselves, which are always the most convincing. Let me repeat: sycophants increase their influence through flattery, by feeding on your psychological insecurity and helping you lie to yourself.

The Servant-Leader archetype, more than any of the others that follow, requires understanding the inner workings of human nature and knowing what the situation demands of you. This goes back to situational awareness, which is a lot more than reading the field. It must include an assessment of the strengths and weaknesses of all participants in the situation, as well as a rigorous self-assessment. Here you must find a balance; you must allow yourself to be guided by the external environment (the extrovert's orientation) without violating the universal laws that govern your behavior (the introvert's orientation). As Plato said, there are factions within you at war with one another, and you must *not* make compromises with yourself. You must remain true to your principles, and live up to the demands of *the ideal self*. In other words, the Servant-Leader must fight and win the revolution within.

Type 2: The Rebel

When I was working on my doctoral dissertation, a psychologist acquaintance paid me a backhanded compliment. He admired me, he said, because politics is the most complex field of study—except, of course, for psychology. *What could possibly be more complicated than the human mind?* he asked rhetorically. He sat back beaming with pride, but didn't get to enjoy it very long. What could be more complicated than the human mind? *Two human minds*, that's what. Would you like to make it more complicated? Add a little diversity—in terms of gender, culture, language, ethnicity, and nationality—and then put them in an environment where resources are scarce and power is asymmetrical, and you can sit back and watch as things become exponentially complicated.

This anecdote sets up the second archetype, the Rebel: equally as important as the Servant-Leader, but oppositional. In the first archetype, I described the cue-giving/cue-taking relationship between the leader and follower. In this archetype, the leader is still giving a cue, but the response is very different. Just as political behavior is hardwired into the species, so is the tension of opposites, also known as the counter-principle.[29] This competitive structure of paired opposites, in which every element (or subsystem) is countervailing and equivalent to its opposite, is necessary to maintain the natural equilibrium of all complex systems, including social and political systems. Complementary (or paired) opposites are like the solstice and the equinox, which moderate and counter-balance one another. This is why politics involves (and even requires) at least two *oppositional* people. In politics, having an adversary is not an inconvenience but a requirement.

The idea that politics is naturally oppositional—a process of change based on the divergence and convergence of opposing forces—means that an overabundance of one force will inevitably produce its opposite. This process begins when the system gets stuck or encounters some sort of impossible situation. And the way to overcome the problem is to increase the system's capacity, and learn new "emergent" behaviors at a higher level.[30] Every system has its own cycles and rhythms of negative and positive, loss and gain, darkness and light, as well as its own evolutionary timetable for when to outgrow its old ways.

As stated, a certain amount of political conflict and opposition is inevitable, and the Rebel personifies this inevitability. What is a rebel? According to Albert Camus, a rebel is someone who first says no, but then says yes as soon as he begins to think for himself. When the Rebel's conscience is awakened and the Rebel begins to think for himself, it means he is becoming a self-determining agent guided by his own moral authority rather than the commands and principles of others. (If you recall, Iyer defined political individuation as the internalization of authority, which also characterizes this archetype.) The Rebel "asserts himself for the sake of everyone in the world when he comes to the conclusion that a command has infringed on something inside him," said Camus.[31] This *something* does not belong entirely to the Rebel; it belongs to human nature and thus belongs to everyone, even the people who insult and abuse him.

It may seem ironic, but coalition-building is an important element of this archetype. Why? Real leaders and followers can't exist in isolation. More often—much more often—we are all members of many groups and factions and multiple overlapping networks. Faced with a power differential that is so asymmetrical that no single individual could hope to present an equivalent countervailing force, people naturally join political parties, labor unions, special interest groups, neighborhood associations, new churches, and even new countries. Acceptance and a sense of belonging are among the primitive, instinctive drives of the collective element, and are not limited to American culture or to modern society in general. These drives are consistent with the sense of belonging (from Maslow's Hierarchy of Values) and also consistent with the latent causes of factionalism, which, as we know, James Madison believed were inherent in human nature.

The Rebel responds to the need for acceptance and a sense of belonging. Like the Servant-Leader, the Rebel must also demonstrate situational awareness, but with a particular emphasis on the strengths and weaknesses of the personalities involved and the likelihood that personal intervention will determine the outcome. In particular, the Rebel is hyper-aware of the factors that prevent people from coming together. If this seems obvious to some readers, forgive me, but sometimes the solution is not to add what is lacking, but to overcome the forces of disunity.

In Chapter 5, I mentioned the network of mutuality, a phrase Martin Luther King Jr. used in his 1963 "Letter from Birmingham Jail." We are all caught in "an inescapable network of mutuality," he said, and thus, "Whatever affects one directly, affects all indirectly." My point: there will be a dominant faction and an opposition faction, a dominant leader and an opposition leader, but because of the tendency to split into factions, combined with the basic human need for belonging, factions will self-organize no matter what you do.

So the Rebel is someone who first says no but eventually says yes. What makes her say no? She refuses to accept reality. And what makes her say yes? She recognizes the art of the possible; that is, she recognizes the conditions and constraints that make her first choice unavailable without losing sight of her second choice. Simply put, the Rebel says yes to an alternative, creative vision of the future. Almost any alternative vision of the future will cause tension, especially among people with a vested interest in maintaining the status quo, because creativity is simultaneously disruptive and constructive.[32] The dissonance between reality (who and where we are) and our vision (what we want) naturally generates tension, which can be a source of destruction and perpetual conflict, but also a source of tremendous growth.[33] As I said in Chapter 3, power opposes other forms of power, and this tension is the motive power of human evolution.

If we could borrow the phrase "creative destruction" from Joseph Schumpeter for a moment, and place the words on a spectrum with creativity on one side and destruction on the other, the Rebel's task would be to transform tension into creative tension. You could argue that the exercise of power inevitably creates tension. This is one way to think about it. Another way is to reverse the cause and effect—that is, tension is natural and predictable in any organization. Tension leads to political behavior. The greater the tension, in terms of disagreement and opposition, in terms of the wishes of one person relative to the behavior of another, the greater motivation there is to engage in political behavior.[34] As James Madison said, ambition is made to counteract ambition.

In general, however, people have a low tolerance for tension and make no distinction between emotional tension and creative tension. This is another opportunity to extend your sense of objectivity. Why? Creative tension is not an emotion and does not necessarily *feel* like anything, certainly nothing like anxiety, sadness, or depression. If creativity is a basic instinct along with hunger and sexuality, then, like the political instinct, it is given to all of us. This means that creativity (like politics) is not the exclusive domain of great personalities. This also means we should not confuse creativity with artistic aptitude, nor should we divide humanity into two groups and argue that creative people are special somehow and thus outside the laws of human nature.[35]

If you are leading an organized opposition, the key factor of success is to find the group's center of attention. I have often heard people use the mathematical analogy "lowest common denominator," which is a useful device for comparing sets of fractions. It is a false analogy for politics, in addition to being cynical and insulting. Your goal should be to locate the group's center of power by identifying the center of attention. The more the focus of attention is limited to a single individual, the more likely that particular individual plays a dominant role in the group.[36] The reason I say "likely" is that there may be more than one center of attention. Where there is more than one center of attention, there will be discord, jealousy, and depravity, and thus factions within factions.

Now, there may be a very good reason to have a single focus of attention: for example, to communicate and coordinate any number of socially beneficial activities. Just because freedom of association is a basic human right, however, doesn't make it efficient. Nonetheless, identifying the center of attention to locate the center of power is (mostly) consistent with our definition of power as *anything that facilitates control of one human over another*. The reason I say "mostly consistent" is because politics is about power, not attention. In addition to identifying the center of attention, you should also look for the group's least obvious leader. Such individuals may not be the most vocal, but when they speak, they do so with moral authority. Look for signs of give-and-take, the subtle leadership cues, and the group's positive response. If you can win the approval of the least obvious leader, then others will accept you and welcome you into the circle.

Before you can lead any group, however, you must join it. You cannot accomplish this through your own will, but only by invitation. Only after you have attained admission to the group will you be able to see and understand its inner workings. This is especially important when people are ready for change, ready for a new direction and new leadership. You may be tempted to encourage the group to make a complete break with the past, but this is almost always a mistake. Severing important links to the past and showing disrespect for your predecessors is one sure way to invite the same contempt from your successors when your time is up. Let your immediate goal be to place yourself not at the top of the group, but at the center—and not simply the center today, but the center that connects the future to the past.

This depends on self-selection rather than control. Consider, for example, prisons, state mental hospitals, and public schools, where there is little or no self-selection. Judges, legislators, boards, and accreditation agencies have control over selection decisions as well as selection (or admission) criteria. Compare this to any volunteer organization that relies on self-selection to attract members. That is, membership is based on "selective entry," and potentially troublesome individuals remove themselves by not seeking entry rather than have the organization refuse to admit them.[37] Self-selection is another way to describe a follower's positive response to a leadership cue.

This presents a particular challenge for the Rebel archetype because people in opposition factions take pride in placing themselves outside conventional society. Their exclusivity, ideological rigidity, and exaggerated behavior can take on the characteristics of a cult, especially after extended periods in opposition. You need to incorporate yourself, not in the legal sense, obviously, but in terms of enlarging your mission and setting goals that will outlive you—that is, unless your goal is to become a member of the permanent opposition. Remember, one of your political goals should be to transcend the limitations of your bureaucratic authority and increase your moral authority. In contemporary English, we call this your legacy. Your leadership, whether you lead a large organization, a small department, or an opposition faction, may transcend your time in office and even your life on earth. If you doubt this, just think of the power that leaders such as Abraham Lincoln and Franklin Roosevelt (and to some extent Ronald Reagan) continue to have long after their deaths.

As stated, Gandhi consistently looked at politics from the perspective of the rebel rather than the ruler. What if we reversed this and looked at politics from the perspective of the ruler? How would you see the Rebel? How would you respond to rebellion? Any effective response would require you to define the opposition—literally to choose your opponent, but also to choose the principles, policies, and strategies that distinguish you from your opponent. The key factor of success is selective unity rather than all-inclusive unity. In other words, invite anyone, welcome everyone, but do not go chasing after those who are reluctant to follow. Even if you persuade people with whom you are in fundamental disagreement to join your coalition, it will disintegrate.

George Washington had some great advice on this topic. If you recall from your high school civics class, Washington said you should never make permanent friends or permanent enemies. Why? Because affection for your friends could blind you to the gap between your interests and theirs, while animosity toward your enemies could blind you to mutual interests you share. The challenge for the Rebel is to remember that politics is the art of the possible, not the art of the perfect, and not to allow old friendships or old enmities become permanent or rigid. The challenge for everyone else is to remember that rebellion is hard-wired into the species and politics is naturally oppositional.

Type 3: The Mentor

It was difficult to choose the name for this archetype because there just isn't a perfect word in English, but I believe "Mentor" is the best of the various alternatives I considered. Would it surprise you to learn the Mentor archetype comes from Greek mythology? The original Mentor was a friend and counselor of Odysseus (also known as Ulysses), hero of Homer's epic poem *Odyssey*. The archetypal Mentor is the wise and trustworthy advisor, always accessible and responsible, who gives the protégé her full attention and her honest opinion.

Although mentor-protégé relationships often develop spontaneously, many organizations now have formal mentoring programs for new employees to help guide their career development because people have discovered the mentor-protégé relationship is beneficial for both parties. Mentors get a great deal of satisfaction seeing others apply their accumulated wisdom, while their protégés acquire access to networks, observe decision-making firsthand, get inside information rarely found in the institution's written record, and learn how to recognize faceless and invisible adversaries.

The mentor-protégé relationship is analogous to the old tutorial method at Oxford University, in which an apprentice/scholar pursued a course of study under the guidance of a senior scholar who assigned coursework, provided feedback, and monitored progress. With no way to hide in the back row, the protégé had no choice but to contribute to the dialogue, which made the tutorial method extremely rigorous. The goal was twofold: to master the topic of inquiry and develop the protégé's ability to think logically and communicate clearly. The Big Brothers/Big Sisters program is based on this idea and matches up mentors with at-risk youths to help little brothers and sisters stay in school, do better in school, stay away from drugs and alcohol, and get along better with their families.

There is something very powerful about mentoring relationships, which may explain why the archetype is replicated in many different situations. Psychologist Richard Brislin wrote, "Native healers pass on the secrets of plants, bishops give selected younger priests advice on combining financial soundness with saving souls, full professors pass on unwritten lore concerning how best to work with the editors of prestigious journals; and CEOs pass on their extensive networks."[38] Business leaders, professional athletes, entertainers, and especially politicians rely on the services of a mentor to help manage their companies, their careers, or their political campaigns. George W. Bush had Dick Cheney, Karen Hughes, Condoleezza Rice, and Karl Rove. Bill Clinton also had several, including James Carville, George Stephanopoulos, and Vernon Jordan Jr., as well as Dick Morris, the Republican pollster Clinton used to execute his triangulation strategy and help him win a second term in office.

In Japan, the role of mentor is played by the *sensei*, which literally means "one who came before." *Sensei* is a formal and respectful title, which refers not only to teachers but also to authority figures and other skilled professionals. The French have their own way of describing this role: éminence *grise*, literally "the gray eminence," who facilitates, mediates, negotiates—and thus acquires great influence over important decisions. Although the gray eminence is the ultimate insider, the position is more complex and precarious than you would guess simply by reading the organizational chart because the gray eminence is not simply a job title, but also a specific kind of relationship.

When I think about the gray eminence, the word that comes to mind is *inconspicuous*. The gray eminence is like a steady, gentle breeze, which does not blow very strong but blows consistently in the same direction. You can see the results of such a breeze when you observe the evergreen trees along the coast in San Francisco's Golden Gate Park, which are sculpted and twisted into the most fascinating forms. My point: for the mentor, power is the result of subtle influence and the accumulation of many small successes. Such successes are not prominent, do not attract attention, do not appear unusual or out of the ordinary, and may be imperceptible to the naked eye, but you can accomplish great things without upsetting the equilibrium when you accumulate small successes through consistent effort.

This role is a privileged position, but dependent on the relationship with the power-holder, and not autonomous. The role of sensei, gray eminence, or consigliere (whatever you call it) depends on a relationship of mutual interest and mutual confidence. Let me give you an example from a scene in *The Godfather*, which takes place in Los Angeles when consigliere Tom Hagen (played by Robert Duvall) meets studio head Jack Woltz (played by John Marley). Hagen's assignment is to convince Woltz to cast Johnny Fontane (Vito Corleone's godson) in his new movie. After Hagen quietly and politely makes his pitch, he receives this abusive rebuttal: "Johnny Fontane will never get that movie! I don't care how many daigo guinea WOP greaseball gumbahs come out of the woodwork!"[39] Hagen replies that he's German-Irish, not Italian, but as you watch the scene unfold, it is clear Woltz's insults mean nothing to Hagen, who even has the poise to tell Woltz he's a fan of his movies.

In the next scene, Woltz has invited Hagen for dinner after he discovers Hagen works for The Godfather, Vito Corleone. Although Woltz still refuses to cast Fontane in his movie and insults Hagen again, Hagen never loses his temper, never raises his voice, and even thanks Woltz for the "very pleasant evening." The next morning, of course, Woltz awakens to find the severed head of his prized race-horse in bed beside him, but this is beside the point. My point is you have to have a thick skin to cope with criticism, hostility, and insults. If you yearn too much for public recognition, it will undermine your effectiveness. The key is to be satisfied with the personal recognition you receive from your client, which is the standard of success for this archetype.

Let me give you another example from Hollywood to convey the cultural and historical scope of this archetype. You may remember the mysterious and disarmingly cheerful Oracle from *The Matrix* movies (first played by Gloria Foster), whom the character Neo (Keanu Reeves) consults to find out if he is "the One." In ancient Greece, an oracle may have been a living person, a god, a building (such as a temple), or an artifact with special powers of prophecy, but in *The Matrix* the Oracle smokes cigarettes, bakes cookies, and looks like someone's grandmother. "You're the Oracle?" says Neo. "Bingo," she says.[40] And what advice does the Oracle give to Neo? *Know thyself*, which in micropolitics means: understand the primitive, instinctive elements hardwired into the entire species; understand the powerful influence of cultural conditioning; and understand yourself—in that order.

The Wachowski siblings (who wrote and directed *The Matrix*) certainly know their Greek mythology. *Know thyself* is an ancient adage, which was allegedly carved into the temple that housed the Oracle at Delphi (located near Mount Parnassus in central Greece), which was considered by many to be the navel of the earth. People living in the region would consult the Oracle at Delphi before any major endeavor. The trouble was the oracle's advice wasn't always clear. And it always required interpretation by the recipient of the advice, as King Croesus of Lydia discovered when he misinterpreted the oracle's prophecy and launched a military campaign against the Persian Empire, which led to his death and the destruction of his kingdom.

The Oracle in *The Matrix* is a computer model—a very so-phisticated computer model to be sure—but nothing more than an "oracle machine," which can predict the most likely event but cannot predict the future. Similarly, you can use computer models to play "what if" games to aid your decision-making, but this is no substitute for a mentor with *the mind of a strategist*.[41] When I say *strategist*, I mean more than someone who plans for the future. I mean someone who knows how to read the field and calculate the power differential; someone who challenges you and exposes the flaws in your thinking and helps you overcome your tunnel vision and narrow-mindedness.

A good strategist (like a good mentor) also plays the role of strategic broker, who does not merely offer advice but is someone you can call on to serve as intermediary, and who can negotiate a settlement on your behalf. Once again, Tom Hagen, consigliere to the Corleone family in *The Godfather*, is the archetypal broker/mentor. After the failed assassination attempt on Vito Corleone, the consigliere is called upon to broker a deal and make peace between the warring families because, as one character says, Tom is not in "the muscle-end of the family." In this context, the power broker is a mentor and a facilitator, who has a reputation for honesty and impartiality, who can identify the people who have the most to gain from working together, get them whatever resources they need, and then get out of the way.[42]

A good factual example of the archetypal strategist/broker/mentor is Henry Kissinger, who for several years served as Richard Nixon's secretary of state and national security advisor, which in-dicates the scope of Kissinger's involvement across the administra-tion. "Kissinger's influence was *extensive*," wrote Robert Greene. "He got himself involved in so many aspects and departments of the administration that his involvement became a card in his hand."[43] This made Kissinger indispensable to Nixon, which made him many friends and enemies, and gave Kissinger a *Svengali*-like reputation. Perhaps you have heard that term before. Svengali was a character in George du Maurier's 1894 gothic horror novel "Trilby." The title character Trilby was a beautiful young woman who worked part-time as a model in mid-19th-century Paris. Svengali was the hypnotist who put Trilby under his spell, and transformed her into a successful singer even though Trilby was tone-deaf. One fateful day, Trilby could not perform because Svengali became ill and could not hypnotize her. The audience booed Trilby off the stage. In time, the term *Svengali* came to describe anyone who exerts too much influence or control over someone else. It is a pejorative term synonymous with any overly influential coach, mentor, or movie director who believes that he—and only he—can draw the best out of an athlete or performer.

The story of Trilby and Svengali highlights the downside with this archetype: The trouble is, no matter how influential or powerful the mentor becomes, the position is inherently precarious because your proximity to power and your relationship with your client are practically interchangeable. Proximity is important because it enhances your influence. Besides, it is hard to give high-value advice if you cannot appreciate or communicate the flaws in your client's thinking. Most importantly, proximity helps give you the executive perspective, and allows you to see alternative courses of action *as if* you were sitting in the big chair. For the Mentor to succeed, she needs to stay out of the big chair—and out the seat of power. Perhaps this goes without saying, but because the mentor's success depends on the client's success, the mentor must choose her clients carefully, and screen them for signs of arrogance, conceit, greed, depravity, dogmatism, vanity, and of course venality.

Speaking of venality, perhaps the world's most famous (but not so successful) mentor/consigliere was Niccolò Machiavelli. Today,

Machiavelli is famous as an author, not a consigliere, because his shrewd advice to the Prince of Florence in the 16th century was unsolicited and unnoticed. There is a chapter in Machiavelli's *The Prince* in which he elaborates on whether it is better to be loved or feared, and concludes it is most advantageous to be both loved and feared, but if you could not be both, it was better to be feared.[44] This cliché has become synonymous with "Machiavellian" politics, which permits (and even promotes) acting based on expediency to the exclusion of morality.

How does this compare with the *first principles* from Chapter 2? As stated, politics has its own peculiar logic, which acknowledges the potential contradiction between political action and morality. This requires you to distinguish political action from morality and to consider the ethical implications of political action. Different political actions have different ethical implications, which you should take into account. Thinking and acting in terms of politics does not exempt you or anyone else from behaving ethically. This principle applies to you in the role of political mentor, strategist, and broker the same as it applies to the role of political actor. In micropolitics, there is no double standard. No exceptions.

You have to remember, Machiavelli was writing for heads of 16th-century Italian principalities, which had different ways of measuring success and different standards of conduct than 21st-century organizations. In the section on the Servant-Leader, I mentioned that false leaders are easy to recognize because, among others things, they are weak, psychologically insecure, and unable to overcome their own fears. Fear is a pervasive force because it is rooted to human nature, but this does not mean you should rely on fear, threats, intimidation, or coercion. One of W. Edwards Deming's famous 14 points for managers was to *drive out fear*. Deming was the ultimate management consultant/consigliere, and argued forcefully that people who are fearful will not give their best performance and cannot learn new skills and knowledge. Fear hurts productivity, hinders teamwork, and leaves people feeling used and abused.[45]

Finally, fear distorts your sense of objectivity and distorts the way you learn, the way you communicate, and the way you respond to the world around you.

Given that fear is pervasive in politics and rooted in human nature, is there any antidote? The short answer is yes, but I must defer to past master Raghavan Iyer on this topic. The antidote to fear, said Iyer, is *thinking things through*. Your fears are connected to, and in every case tested by your fear of death.[46] Now, I will acknowledge that different people have different fears—large and small—which come from many different sources. Perhaps you have no fear of death, but are squeamish about politics. Perhaps, as I said in the Preface, you have hemophobia—an irrational fear of the sight of blood. Whatever your fear, the antidote is *thinking things through*.

When you think things through to their logical conclusion, you can take hold of your life, give it direction and meaning, and make a mockery of your fears. As Albus Dumbledore told young Harry Potter, *Death is nothing but the next great adventure for the well-organized mind.*[47] The ability to question everything, take nothing for granted, and think a problem through in any direction is evidence of a well-organized mind. Suggesting that no one may claim self-mastery who has not learned to overcome their fear of death would be too much, perhaps, but overcoming your fears is a prerequisite for becoming ruler of your inner world. If you had a protégé, would this be something you would want to teach her? If you had a mentor, would this be something you would want to learn from her?

A final word of advice: For the would-be mentor, success requires caution and reserve, and depends on never forgetting your subordinate position. Success depends not on your ability to attract attention to yourself, but on your ability to produce the maximum positive outcome for your client or protégé. Because the role is relatively defenseless, you should work discreetly and tactfully behind the scenes in order to maintain your client's confidence. You must take care to remain free from any conflict of interest, financial or otherwise, which would compromise your relationship and thus your proximity to power. It will be impossible to master the Mentor archetype if you are too submissive or too assertive. The consequences of your work should be more conspicuous than you are. Avoid extravagance and leave fame to others.

Type 4: The Recluse

The Bible (Genesis 2:1-30) says God created heaven and the earth, divided darkness from light, divided the waters, created the seasons, filled the world with plants, animals, and all kinds of living creatures, and then created human beings, all in six days. Finally she said, "Behold!" She ended her work on the seventh day and rested. I am not proselytizing, just trying to make a point. The day God rested from her work—the seventh day—is the day she blessed and sanctified. What does this tell us? Just this: only by withdrawing did God allow the world to come into being. Creation is divine, but so is intelligent self-restraint because it allows your creation to come into being.

According to principle No. 3 (from Chapter 2), power is anything that facilitates control. However, the most significant attribute of this archetype is withdrawing from politics and giving up the fantasy that you are in control.[48] The key to the Recluse archetype is to conserve energy by retreating. Your retreat takes place on the surface, while on the interior it is possible and necessary to construct a virtual mansion where you can cultivate your moral authority and spiritual freedom. This virtual mansion is the staging area where your training and self-development are ongoing. The Recluse does not yield, but distances herself from her adversary, putting herself out of reach. This is not an act of rebellion (see Archetype 2: the Rebel) but an act of disengagement. There is no violence or even anger associated with this type, but a quiet determination to limit your involvement.[49] If you recall what I said in Chapter 1, this is the kind of cool, scientific detachment you see in the forensic pathologist or medical examiner.

Whatever unpleasant experience you are facing, you must not permit confrontational people to turn you away from your principles. Confrontational people may be masters of micropolitics, and may be counting on your reclusion from politics to impose their will. It is much more likely, however, that such people know no other way to relate to people. This is one of the reasons why political conflict is inherent in human nature. However, just because conflict is inevitable (and thus predictable) does not mean you should invite it or rush toward it. It is easy to lose patience when your goal is in sight. It is also easy to deceive yourself into thinking the situation demands personal intervention, and calls for you to take the shortest, straightest path toward your goal. Sometimes, you need to emulate a hermit who withdraws from the world, offering nothing, seeking nothing. This does not mean contemplating your navel, but examining the effect you have on the world around you and saving yourself for future challenges.

Remember, micropolitics is not a solitary but a social skill, which implies interdependence among the participants. In our modern society, it is hard to shut yourself off from the world to seek renewal and to incubate your political animal. For some people, particularly those who have trouble disconnecting from the Internet, putting the Recluse archetype into practice will be difficult. But do not worry because emulating a hermit or recluse is just a metaphor. That is, you do not need to move to a remote mountaintop without WiFi, cable television, or cell phone service. However, you do need to cultivate a capacity for professional detachment.

Professional detachment is the opposite of emotional investment. For lawyers, this means representing your clients without prejudging them. For doctors, nurses, and social workers, it means not permitting yourself to become emotionally involved with patients, clients, and cases. Non-attachment does not mean you lose touch with people or lose the ability to enjoy other people. It is okay to take an interest in the affairs of others as long as you do not intrude. When you inhabit the Recluse archetype, you should act as you would if you were a stranger in town or perhaps a good neighbor: friendly but not overeager, helpful but not intrusive; you call out a greeting rather than insisting on a lengthy conversation; you do not cause offense or forget to return a favor.

In the course of your personal and professional life, you will find yourself in difficult situations. If you are ambitious, you may safely assume that your ambitions will interfere with someone else's ambitions and vice versa. As stated, an important element of mastering micropolitics is situational awareness, reading the field in the current situation while anticipating the future situation. That is only half of it—because micropolitics is a social skill. The other half means knowing when to yield, when to resist, and when to go on offense. And then, it starts all over again because you have to evaluate the effects of your own performance with the same objectivity as you would evaluate anybody else's. How will you know when your journey is complete? How will you know when to quit?

Your success with the Recluse archetype depends on timing, by regulating the pace of events to achieve your goal, and there are two ways to do this. The first is the way a dancer's movements match the accompanying music. The second is the way a composer (or musician) increases or decreases the tempo of the music. Successful dancers, musicians, comedians, performing artists—and all successful politicians—understand the subtleties of using rhythm and tempo to reach the audience and create an emotional response at exactly the right moment. It is important to know when momentum has naturally completed its cycle, which is a prerequisite for knowing when to stop. Remember, your goal is more complex than total victory. Achievement of your goal should be as economical as possible, meaning you should use your scarce resources wisely and minimize waste. Taking political action can be exciting, and it can be tempting to go too far. To avoid overrunning your tactics, you need to harmonize your tactics to the demands of the time. Micropolitics depends on movement and stillness, moving when it is time to move and keeping still when it is time to keep still.

The Recluse must learn to be patient. The implication, as I have emphasized elsewhere, is that emotional self-control (overcoming that awful fear) is an important element of micropolitics. Emotionalism is particularly self-destructive because it distracts from your long-term goals, prevents the entrance of reason, and clouds your ability to differentiate between political actions and petty revenge fantasies. In micropolitics, it is imperative that you master this element. Think of kryptonite, which, as any fan of comic books will tell you, comes from Krypton, the home planet of Superman. Kryptonite is the debris that remains from the planet's destruction in a nuclear chain reaction—and is the only thing harmful to Superman. In micropolitics, the analogous thing is emotionalism.

Besides, is there anything more wasteful than a temper tantrum? Unfortunately, we are all susceptible to losing our temper for trivial reasons. Anger combines with other primary emotions (such as fear and sadness) and coalesces into larger and more complex emotions, which cloud your mind, exaggerate and falsify your perceptions, and hinder self-mastery. You probably already know how difficult it can be to subdue yourself when your mind is racing, but this is another test of self-mastery. Your composure must come naturally because you cannot induce tranquility by force. Your goal—to borrow a line from George Washington—is to refrain from foreign entanglements. When you face an adversary with a clear power advantage, keep traveling and do not tempt fate. If your adversary has a power advantage, do not confront her but execute a calm and controlled retreat. Thus, emulating the Recluse is not weakness but wisdom.

As stated, archetypes are symbols in concentrated form, and all the archetypes in micropolitics are human forms in particular. To help explain this archetype, I would like to change the perspective. Instead of examining the Recluse, let's become the Recluse. Now, close your eyes and open them. Where are you? You're in prison—inside the ultimate instrument of power.[50] Consider how much power the prison exerts over you. It has the power to confine you, control your body, deprive you of your freedom, observe you, and catalog your behavior. A prison would decide (for days, months, and years on end) when you ate, as well as how much and how often. A prison would decide—if not when you slept and when you awoke—the appropriate time you should sleep and when you should wake up. If you were a prisoner, you would see the prison as ultimate instrument of power.

What makes a prison so powerful? I don't mean visually now. I mean to ask, what are the "first principles" of prisons, and can we list them like the first principles of politics in Chapter 2? Yes we can, with a little help from French philosopher Michel Foucault. First among these, according to Foucault, is the need to isolate you (the prisoner) from the external environment, and this means everything good and bad. Isolation guarantees maximum power over you and therefore total submission. Isolation forces you into solitude, which for most people (sociable people) is punishment. Isolation creates a barrier and thus removes you from society. Isolation imposes monastic discipline, forcing you to confront yourself, listen to your conscience, and contemplate your existence. Isolation also offers the opportunity for rehabilitation, at least in theory.[51]

For the ordinary individual, isolation would be punishment. For those who have achieved a certain degree of self-mastery, however, this is a reward. This is seclusion and solitude. For the Recluse this is a playground, which offers unlimited opportunities for reflection, self-development, and ultimately individuation. The downside of reclusiveness is that it reinforces the status quo. Thus, you should make choosing to emulate the Recluse a fully conscious choice rather than a habit, and be prepared to suffer the consequences of reclusion and isolation. In this context, suffering is not a sacrifice—because there is no place in micropolitics for martyrs.

Regardless of the situation, act as if you regard success and failure with equal detachment and skepticism. Learn to control your thoughts and emotions as you read the field and probe for weakness in your opponent, and prepare yourself to take action (defensive or offensive) at all times. Sometimes, this looks exactly like doing nothing, which makes it one of the greatest challenges for people accustomed to leading and taking action. An example of this is the composed response President Barack Obama displayed during the recent uprising in Iran following the fraudulent election in 2009 and again during the protests in Egypt and Libya in 2011. Obama's critics urged him to say or do more (including military intervention) to show the country's solidarity with the protesters. Obama's self-restraint reminded me of George H.W. Bush and James Baker when the Berlin Wall fell in 1989 and later on when the Soviet Union disintegrated. In situations such as these, the best thing is also the most difficult thing: disciplined non-intervention.

For people accustomed to taking action, sitting in stillness and submitting to the conditions of the time can be a monumental challenge. Sadly, too few people have the political acumen to recognize such crucial moments *while in the moment*. One of the challenges of this archetype is limiting your thoughts to the situation at hand. In general, it is wise to identify potential problems beyond your control, consider the worst-case scenario, and develop an alternative course of action, also known as "Plan B." However, too much contingency planning can be demoralizing and ultimately self-defeating. Keeping your goal firmly in mind will prevent you from drifting and vacillating. Keeping your goal in mind while cultivating self-control and self-discipline will prevent you from acting before the time is right.

Finally, this archetype highlights the importance of maintaining a well-ordered inner attitude, one in which you do not let your thoughts wander and create a situation of chronic discontent. Sometimes, a great spirit remains unrecognized, and does not permit society's provisional standards to determine success or failure. Instead of playing a role in public life or embarking on the hero's journey, you should learn to resist the temptation to plunge ahead. You must not fear you are wasting time or losing time because you're not really losing anything. If you free yourself from vanity—which is always easier said than done—you will be able to conceal your abilities and avoid attracting unwanted attention. Always keep your goal in sight but learn to hold back. Cultivate the ability to desist, and the ability to recognize moments of crucial political significance while you are simultaneously cultivating your emotional self-control. If you follow the path of the holy sage, seeking solitude and withdrawing into seclusion, you can explore your options and prepare your next step.

Type 5: The Judo Master

To introduce this archetype, let's imagine a scenario in which there is a power differential between two people—between a supervisor and a subordinate, for example. On a power scale of 1 to 10, let's say the supervisor has 10 units of power and the subordinate has 5. If the supervisor exerts all of her power and the subordinate all of hers, the supervisor will prevail. However, instead of resisting, suppose the subordinate pulls when the supervisor pushes. The subordinate's power increases far beyond the limits of her position, and the supervisor loses her balance. This highlights an old Japanese expression derived from jujitsu: *softness controls hardness*. What does this mean in practice? Confrontation causes defeat. If you oppose power with power, the one with more power will win. Instead, you should look for leverage and consider alternative methods to accomplish your goals. This is the skillful use of power. This is the gentle way.

The name of this archetype comes from judo, which is a modern variation of unarmed combat created in late 19th-century Japan by Kano Jigoro (1860–1938). In Japanese, *ju* means "gentle" or "to yield," and *dō* means "way" or "principle." Translated literally, *judo* means "the gentle way." The principle of giving way or gentleness does not mean surrendering the initiative, but leveraging force rather than resisting it. When an aggressor pushes, you pull; when she pulls, you push. Judo is the art and practice of using your adversary's power to your advantage in order to gain victory, and is thus defensive rather than offensive. The fundamental principle, and the ultimate purpose of this archetype, is to *win without fighting*.

Have you ever noticed how infrequently people with martial arts training get into street fights? This occurred to me as I was reading an article in the *San Francisco Chronicle* about two men who shared an interest in judo. The two men did not know one another and met by accident while waiting at a train station after a Giants baseball game. One man saw the other wearing a judo jacket, approached him, and started up a conversation. The two started sparring (or play fighting) but it escalated somehow. One landed in the hospital and the other landed in jail. According to the deputy district attorney quoted in the news article, the defendant (who happened to be a national judo competitor) lost his self-control and became "more interested in demonstrating his dominance."[52] As I said, this story caught my eye because people with this kind of training seldom engage in this kind of street fighting. However, the district attorney's observation that some people care more about demonstrating their dominance than demonstrating their self-mastery sounded all too familiar.

There is an old adage that suggests sometimes it is best to hide your inner light, not shine too brightly and not reveal too much about yourself. This way, you won't attract unwanted attention. This is one of the keys to the Judo Master. Outwardly, you are modest and compliant. Inwardly, you are patiently waiting for the right moment to ensure your will prevails. You do not rush forward wildly, but quietly cultivate your self-mastery regardless of the turmoil in the world around you. In practice, your actions should be responsive rather than proactive, and begin only when your opponent takes the initiative. Your opponent will often communicate her move beforehand. If you have anticipated the attack, you can maintain your emotional detachment, and simply move out of the way. Good timing and the right attitude make all the difference.

Like any martial artist, you should find your balance before you act and compose your mind before you speak. If your movements are unpredictable, your voice is agitated, and your demands are presumptuous, you will inspire opposition rather than cooperation. However, if you master the principles from Chapter 2, you can assert yourself far beyond the limitations of your position. Why is that? Effective use of this archetype harnesses your adversary's power, combines it with your leverage, and then creates a multiplier effect. This, in turn, moves through the organization: up, down, and across the hierarchy. In this way, you can preempt fear, anger, and other negative emotions from organizing into larger, more destructive systems. The effects may not be immediately evident, but the cumulative effect can be great. The long-term effects of emulating this archetype are the result of persistent influence, and thus hard to reverse by force.

In general, the purpose of micropolitics is to enable weaker people to defend themselves against people who are more powerful. The ultimate goal of this particular archetype is not to prevail in every conflict, nor to demonstrate your dominance, but to preempt conflict before it begins. Furthermore, the Judo Master refrains from engaging in unequal conflict. This applies equally to those more powerful and those less powerful than you, and requires you to be gentle even when (especially when) you are more powerful or influential than your opponent. Gaining mastery over your opponents is not the same as defeating or humiliating them. When you win a victory by applying leverage, which is naturally nonviolent, you use only as much force as required.

Power is a blunt instrument, which you should avoid using except when necessary. When is it necessary? This depends on your understanding of the economy of motion. Applied to micropolitics, it means producing the maximum positive outcome with the least amount of effort. Understanding the economy of motion is important because power is a decisive factor only in short conflicts. The longer a conflict lasts, the more important endurance becomes, which will get you into trouble if you overestimate your power and underestimate your adversary's endurance. Before you take any irreversible action, you should consider whether it is in your best interests to engage in a prolonged conflict. If you have an absolute advantage of power—and if you have no other recourse—you should incapacitate your adversary using as little force as possible. Otherwise, you should conserve your energy, encourage your adversary to dissipate hers, and bide your time.[53]

Because politics is a social skill, it requires close and sustained interaction with friends and adversaries alike. Artful practitioners of micropolitics do not need to be ruthlessly and relentlessly cunning, nor do they need to overpower their opponents, even if they could easily do so. During my long career in business, government, and higher education, one of the things I have noticed is the way unskilled executives rely on the authority vested in their office. They believe they deserve respect—and obedience—simply because of the office they hold. That they continue to believe this in an age of nepotism, cronyism, tokenism, and other forms of favoritism is astounding, but they believe it nonetheless.

Artful practitioners of micropolitics do not rely on the authority vested in their office. Instead, they use intelligence, creativity, and technique to accomplish their goals. In this way, the Judo Master can produce a cultural transformation, which is responsive and cooperative, gentle but not weak. This is not an easy task, and certainly not possible except over the long term, but imagine if everyone learned to apply the "the gentle way" to everyone else in the organization no matter how powerful or powerless they were. If, through your example, you convinced people around you to assimilate your behavior, it would exemplify authentic leadership and the subtle effectiveness of conditioned power.

As stated, the relationship between micropolitics and self-mastery often means imposing and enforcing limitations on yourself and others. Sometimes, it is necessary to concentrate your power where you need it most at exactly the right moment. However, direct confrontation is often not the shortest path to success. First, you must calculate the power differential. If your adversary has a clear power advantage, you should not launch a direct attack because the one with more power will prevail. This highlights the importance of situational awareness because achieving the maximum positive outcome depends on acting when it is time for action and waiting when it is time to wait. Of course, you must calculate the risk, the cost, and the benefits of taking political action. The better you understand this, the less likely you are to engage in unequal conflict, and the more likely you are to avoid unnecessary expenditure of energy.

You may wonder if there is any situation in which a direct confrontation is the wiser choice. The answer is yes, when you have a moral or legal obligation (a duty) to put yourself at risk in the service of a higher cause. What is duty? The word is so commonplace it seems to have lost its meaning. According to Gandhi, duty is the willingness to suffer for your beliefs and the refusal to abdicate responsibility.[54] It is easy for emergency responders at the other end of the 911 call to define duty: While others are running out of a burning building, they are running in. For most of us, situations like this do not happen every day, which makes it all the more important to recognize them when they do. For the Judo Master, devotion to duty means following the middle path. On one side is excessive modesty and on the other is overconfidence. Both those paths make the same mistake because there is little difference between an ostentatious display of modesty and an ostentatious display of confidence. The Judo Master walks the middle path—neither flattering those above her nor intimidating those below. Your goal should be modesty in its proper measure, without trying to make any impression other than the results of your work.

I said earlier that *judo* translates literally to "the gentle way." Now I'd like to share something Michel Foucault wrote on the topic. The gentle way, according to Foucault, "is an art of conflicting energies, an art of images linked by association, the forging of stable connections that defy time: it is a matter of establishing the representation of pairs of opposing values, of establishing quantitative differences between the opposing forces, of setting up a complex of obstacle-signs that may subject the movement of forces to a power relation."[55] I'm sharing this because I admire Foucault's political imagination and poetic flourish.

I like poetry, but not as much as I like lists, especially checklists. Lists get to the heart of the matter. Remember Oskar Schindler? For this reason, I listed Hans Morgenthau's principles of political realism at the beginning of Chapter 2. Foucault made a similar list of the principles of punishment, *the gentle way of punishment*. Let's see if we can adapt Foucault's principles the same way we adapted Morgenthau's, squeeze them into the space between us, and see how they relate to this archetype and micropolitics in general.

First, said Foucault, punishments must not be arbitrary. This means punishments must be logical and the link between the crime and the punishment must be obvious. Second, punishments must reverse the "economy of interests" in the criminal's mind. That is, if you highlight the disadvantages of the crime, you can make it less attractive. The idea is to make sure that the fear of the punishment is equal to or greater than any motivation to commit the crime. Third, punishments must have an expiration date. For violent crimes, the proof, judgment, and punishment should be immediate. Punishments for less serious crimes should fit the crime but get gradually more lenient over time, more punitive at the beginning than at the end.

Fourth, punishments must be directed at everyone, not just criminals but potential criminals, and the general public as well. Crimes and punishments must be publicized so that everyone sees the punishments are appropriate, and that the system serves everyone's interests. Fifth, the system of punishment must represent public morality. If there has been a crime, the law must be restated, and the links continuously reinforced among the law, the criminal violation, and the punishment. People must see themselves as part of this system. Sixth, the system of punishments must adhere to a strict economy, which avoids excess—excessive force as well as excessive leniency. The gentle way of punishment must never be used to glorify crime and never to terrorize, but to teach.[56]

I admire the way Foucault's principles highlight and connect various elements of micropolitics: symbolism, the tension of opposites, the importance of political economy, and the idea of *how-much-to*. I'm reminded of something I said in Chapter 4: Self-mastery is a multi-dimensional value system with a feedback loop. I'm also reminded of something I said in Chapter 1: The essential unit of analysis in micropolitics is the individual. In Foucault's principles, the essential unit of analysis is *punishment*, which is an aggregate or "macro" level unit of analysis like power or war, or any other system-wide factor. This is an important difference, but not as important as the similarities.

Every one of Foucault's principles about punishment points to something important about power. That is, you must not use power arbitrarily; you should preempt conflict, if possible; you should refrain from long power struggles; you should try to reform the system; you should conform to the highest ethical standards; and you should always avoid the excessive use of force. Remember, *judo* means "the gentle way." The fundamental principle, and the ultimate purpose of this archetype, is to win without fighting. You won't have a full set of tools if you don't master this archetype. And you need a full set so that you don't rely on power. You also need to know which tool to reach for first.

There's one more thing about this archetype, and it has to do with the tactical self, which we discussed in Chapter 5. As stated, micropolitics does not require a lot of showmanship. However, there are situations when it may work to your advantage to create the appearance of submission and the illusion of weakness to confuse your adversary, so she cannot fathom your real intent. However, putting on a show of confusion, incompetence, or timidity in order to encourage your adversary's over-confidence can be difficult (or even impossible) for highly educated people or those who have built a career on intellectual prowess. To make your show of humility convincing, you must overcome your fear of appearing confused, incompetent, or weak.

This reminds me of a clever line from *Reversal of Fortune*, the 1990 movie adaptation of Alan Dershowitz's book about the conviction and later acquittal of socialite Claus von Bülow (masterfully played by Jeremy Irons) who was accused of attempting to murder his wife. In one scene, Dershowitz interrupts von Bülow during a game of backgammon. "Most people think it's a game of luck," says Claus. "Actually, it's largely a matter of nerve."[57] Mastering this archetype is like winning at backgammon: It requires some luck but mostly strategy, flexibility, and not losing your nerve.

Remember, the closer two people are in terms of their bureaucratic authority, the more likely that politics will determine the outcome. Because you are not easily intimidated—or at least you can put on a good show—you will not automatically take up a counter-position. Because you know not to arouse suspicion in your adversaries, you know how to avoid direct confrontation. Because you know power is decisive only in short conflicts—and you do not rely on power anyway—you will preempt conflict and prevent fear, anger, and other negative emotions from organizing into larger, more destructive systems. As I said at the beginning of this archetype, *softness controls hardness*. This is the gentle way.

Type 6: The Resister

To introduce this archetype, let me echo the words of Raghavan Iyer, who envisioned a future in which leaders exemplified moral authority beyond the limits of any bureaucratic structure, and who did so effortlessly and nonviolently.[58] Micropolitics does not condone using or threatening violence, though I acknowledge many books have been written that explicitly portray the workplace and the marketplace as a battlefield. To master micropolitics, you must learn to communicate without appropriating the vocabulary of weapons and warfare. Fortunately, we have some guidance. During many civil rights campaigns in South Africa and India, Mahatma Gandhi advocated nonviolent civil disobedience, and his example inspired many other leaders, particularly Martin Luther King Jr.

Gandhi believed disobedience was a birthright that belonged to every human being, which could never be surrendered without surrendering one's self-respect.[59] He came to dislike the connotations of "passive resistance" and introduced new concepts such as *Ahimsa* (nonviolence) and *Satyagraha* (truth-force) because he believed there was nothing *passive* about nonviolence. Likewise, there is nothing passive about micropolitics. But there is an element of resistance, which is both personal and social. Resistance is a personal act because the resister's primary concern is her own behavior. Resistance may become a social act if it is calculated to change someone else's bad behavior. In any case, the idea is to set a good example, not to impose one's values.[60]

Gandhi came to his beliefs in part by reading Leo Tolstoy's *The Kingdom of God Is Within You*. In Tolstoy's great philosophical study from the late 19th century, he built his argument and the doctrine of non-resistance on the first book of the New Testament, specifically the Sermon on the Mount. "People often think the question of non-resistance to evil by force is a theoretical one, which can be neglected. Yet this question is presented by life itself to all men, and calls for some answer from every thinking man," wrote Tolstoy. "At every new struggle that arises one must inevitably decide; am I, or am I not, to resist by force what I regard as evil."[61] According to Tolstoy, the question of resistance (or non-resistance) arose with the original act of violence, which is documented in the story of Cain and Abel. But ever since the Sermon on the Mount, in which Christ specifically instructed his followers to turn the other cheek, love their enemies, and pray for those who cursed, hated, and persecuted them, there has been a way to withhold your consent *and* avoid violence.

This leads us to another major influence on Gandhi's moral and political philosophy, and another archetypal Resister, the great American philosopher Henry David Thoreau. Gandhi gave credit to Thoreau for coining the phrase "civil disobedience" and considered Thoreau's essay by that name a masterpiece.[62] Thoreau was a firm believer in the motto *The government is best which governs least*. He believed government was a necessary evil because whatever we may have accomplished as a people, we would have done anyway, if only the government had gotten out of the way. Thoreau's idea of civil disobedience was based on the same belief held by the authors of the *Federalist Papers*, that your status as a human being comes first, and is always more meaningful than your role as a citizen of the state.

Thoreau's essay was published in 1849, just one year after Marx and Engels published the *Communist Manifesto*. And more than three million people—10 percent of Americans—were held as slaves according to the 1850 Census. This historical context is important because Thoreau was a staunch abolitionist. When Thoreau said government was evil, however, he did not mean it was always and uniformly evil, as in the case of slavery. He meant government was unworthy of our obedience because no law magically became honorable simply because people obeyed it. He wondered why any citizen should surrender her conscience to the government. If you're just going to surrender it, then why do you even have a conscience? "I think that we should be men [and women] first, and subjects afterward. It is not desirable to cultivate a respect for the law, so much as for the right."[63]

Thoreau's basic idea—which exemplifies an introverted sense of objectivity—was that doing the right thing was more important than obeying the law. To prove the point, Thoreau stopped paying his taxes for several years and was locked up (for one night) as a result. Surrounded by stone walls two feet thick, and a strong door made of iron and wood, Thoreau could not help being struck by the government's foolishness. Then, an idea occurred to him, something he never realized before. The government never intentionally confronts someone's moral authority, only their bodies. Why? It is because the government may be physically superior, but rarely (if ever) morally superior.

Thoreau did not care how his tax dollars were spent, but he did care what effect it might have if he gave his allegiance to an unworthy government. Because the government lacked moral authority, Thoreau simply refused to pledge his allegiance. "There will never be a really free and enlightened State until the State comes to recognize the individual as a higher and independent power, from which all its own power and authority are derived, and treats him accordingly," he wrote.[64] Think about that for a moment. How is the government going to recognize you as a "higher and independent power" if you do not recognize it yourself? That's what makes this archetype so powerful: She does recognize it. And that's not all. She knows she's overpowered, but follows her political conscience and refuses to give her allegiance.

Rosa Parks is a perfect example of this. Before she was a civil rights icon, she was a seamstress in Montgomery, Alabama. She was on her way home from work on a city bus one day and refused to give up her seat to a white passenger. The police arrested her and charged her with violating a law that was (to quote Thoreau) unworthy of our obedience. As I said before, resistance is a personal act because the resister's primary concern is her own behavior. Rosa Parks's refusal to give up her seat began as a personal act and became political when others decided to follow her example (in the Montgomery Bus Boycott). Her personal act became symbolic because it stood for something and projected something larger than itself (see Chapter 5). This is how the seamstress became the archetype.

You may wonder what the difference is between this archetype and the Rebel. The Resister is not necessarily an opposition leader and may not even be a member of any organized opposition. The Resister inhabits a private world of universal principles, waiting patiently for the rest of the world to come around. Her goal is neither to conquer nor to overthrow the system but to teach a lesson, which the Bible (Job 38:11) sums up as follows: *Hitherto shalt thou come, but no farther.* She asserts her moral authority by not giving her consent (See Chapter 4), by refusing to allow her political conscience to atrophy, and by not permitting her government (or her family, community, or employer) to use her as an agent of injustice. She believes in peace, freedom, and social justice, which means she's more like an abolitionist or a civil rights activist than a revolutionary.

Permit me to bring the discussion back down to earth. In Jack London's literary masterpiece *The Call of the Wild,* there is one horrifying scene that conveys the essence of the Resister archetype. In case you never read it, I'll summarize the story for you. The story takes place during the Klondike gold rush. The central character is a dog named Buck, and although he doesn't know it, the gold rush has created a thriving black market for big, long-haired dogs such as him to serve as sled dogs in the Klondike. Buck gets himself kidnapped and sold, and loaded on a northbound train. And this leads to Buck's encounter with the Man in the Red Sweater, the so-called dog doctor whose job is to break Buck's will and turn him into a suitable sled dog.

The horrifying scene—the one that conveys the essence of the Resister archetype—begins at the end of a long journey. After days without food or water, Buck is thirsty and hungry, growling and snarling and determined to attack the nearest target at the first opportunity. As soon as the Man opens the crate, Buck attacks with all his pent-up rage. But the Man is ready because he is the "dog doctor" and smashes Buck to the ground. Buck attacks again and again until he's staggering and exhausted. But the Man isn't finished with him yet. He calmly walks up to Buck and delivers a fierce blow to the snout that knocks him senseless.

Slowly, Buck recovers his senses (but not his strength) and eyes the Man warily as he brings him water and feeds him chunks of meat. This is Buck's first lesson in power and it is a revelation. Buck knows he is defeated and realizes he has no chance against this man or anyone else wielding a club. Many days go by and many other crates arrive containing dogs destined for the Klondike. Buck observes every brutal encounter with the Man in the Red Sweater, and every time, it reinforces this lesson: the man with a club is the master. Eventually, each dog submits to the Man, admits defeat—or dies.[65]

Buck is observant in another way that is so subtle it might escape your notice. Some dogs do not merely admit defeat, but fawn over the Man, wag their tails, and even lick his hand, all of which Buck finds disgusting. The Man in the Red Sweater is master and lawgiver—that is, as long as he wields the club. Although the club compels Buck's submission, he understands the difference between submission and consent. He understands the difference between admitting defeat and accepting it. In the course of your political trials you are sure to encounter defeat—everyone does—but you must understand what Buck understands. His subtle act of resistance, his refusal to wag his tail, was his declaration of independence.

Just as there is a difference between submission and consent, there is a difference between resistance and obstructionism. The guiding principle of obstructionism is simple: *anything but that*, which may be useful when you know what you *don't* want. Resistance, on the other hand, is for those individuals with an introverted sense of objectivity, for those who know where to find the absolutes (see Chapter 2). Universal principles rather than human-made codes of conduct govern her behavior. Resistance is the right to refuse, the right to suffer, but, most importantly, the right to stand alone. Resistance is a birthright of every individual. It is the right to think for yourself, and decide whether to slavishly submit or to declare your independence. Finally, resistance is a personal choice, which becomes a powerful political instrument the moment anyone follows your good example.

Type 7: The Opportunist

It was just as difficult to choose the name for this archetype as it was for Type 3: the Mentor. Knowing how to describe it but not what to call it, I consulted my mother's favorite book: the dictionary. My first choice was "crisis manager," but this seemed too confining. Then I thought of that cliché (maybe it's true) that the words *crisis* and *opportunity* both translate into the same word in Japanese. Anyway, I flipped through the dictionary and found *opportunism*: "The practice or policy of adapting one's actions, judgments, etc. to circumstances, as in politics, in order to further one's immediate interests, without regard for basic principles or eventual consequences."[66] I am not sure to which principles the people who wrote that dictionary were referring, but I think this definition describes the archetype rather well. Indeed, the Opportunist adapts her actions to the circumstances in order to further her interests. However, the last clause about disregarding basic principles or eventual consequences is false, of course. We know from Chapter 2 that micropolitics has its own standards of success, its own peculiar logic, and its own principles.

My other difficulty with this archetype has to do with my preference for explaining micropolitics without appropriating the vocabulary of warfare. But that self-imposed prohibition is pointless here. If we go back to our dictionary definition, we cannot help but see parallels in Sun Tzu's *The Art of War*, which is perhaps the world's oldest discourse on military strategy.[67] Opportunism was his first, and in some ways only principle. Opportunism requires you to take advantage of any helpful or unusual circumstances that might work to your benefit, and modify your tactics accordingly. That's the dictionary definition and the heart and soul of this archetype. My task here is to transform this most militant archetype into a full-fledged political archetype.

Prussian military theorist Carl von Clausewitz considered war an instrument of politics, and a continuation of politics, *by other means*. Although war does not supersede the autonomy of the political sphere, this archetype and the Judo Master are useful for understanding certain laws and principles. One of these is the principle of economy. The martial arts are similar to the healing arts in this respect, in that the solution is inseparable from your understanding of the problem. When it comes to the political arts, the martial arts, and the healing arts, the less you intervene, the better. This is what the principle of economy means. Even though you should always try to intervene as little as possible, this does not mean you can lower your guard or permit your skills to deteriorate. It is as important to be cool and decisive during a crisis as it is to model the virtues you hope others would emulate during moments of relative calm. As a political archetype, this is what makes the Opportunist so powerful because you must marshal your resources the same way: with organization, allocation of resources, and proper discipline.

Advancing your interests requires cultivating a good poker face (a tactical self; see Chapter 5) that does not communicate your true thoughts, feelings, or intentions, and does not give anything away except what you want to give away. Minimally, a good poker face is not just a neutral facial expression, but a contrived facial expression (and body posture) specifically used to prevent other people from figuring out your motives. Optimally—and whenever necessary—you should be able to use your public persona to mislead your adversaries and spread disinformation like any decent intelligence agent. Sometimes, maintaining your false persona will entail giving the impression that you condone wrongdoing, but mastering micropolitics would never require you to take part in any criminal or unethical activity.

The idea of using a tactical self or political persona to conceal your intentions may be too abstract to be useful in your organization, but tactical dislocation is a good practical example of this. Tactical dislocation is a diversionary tactic designed to disrupt your adversary's plans and force them to move out of position, in order to create an opening for you to maneuver. In terms of military doctrine, tactical dislocation refers to pinning down the enemy's main strength—distracting them and weakening them—while you identify and exploit their most vulnerable point. If you have seen the movie about General George S. Patton, then you may remember him describing this as "Hold 'em by the nose and kick 'em in the pants."[68] The real-life Patton wrote many professional articles on warfare, particularly for tanks and other armored vehicles, and dislocation was one of his favorite tactics.

Before WWII, Patton was an Olympic athlete, master swordsman, and instructor on sword fighting and fencing. Patton applied some of the tactics he used in fencing to warfare. In fencing, for example, a feint can be an attack, or a retreat, or any other kind of maneuver that deceives or distracts your adversary. The idea is to mislead your adversary regarding your true intentions. You execute a feint-attack to provoke a defensive reaction, forcing your adversary to concentrate her forces (or resources) in one area while leaving another exposed. You execute a feint-retreat to cause confusion or to draw your adversary into a pre-planned ambush. The feint-attack and feint-retreat are both useful for distracting your adversary and getting her to give up her strong defensive position and move into a vulnerable position.

Using tactical dislocation is analogous to using a political persona. It is nothing but a political technique and no more unethical than gearing up before a game or putting on a uniform before going to work. We see tactical dislocation all the time in sports: in baseball the "change-up" to fool batters; in football the "draw" to fool defenders; and in basketball the "no-look pass" that often fools everyone, players and spectators alike. Former Lakers star Ervin Johnson was the master of this particular diversionary tactic, as he dribbled down the court on a fast break, turning his head one way and flipping the ball to an undefended teammate beside him or even behind him.

In terms of micropolitics, dislocation is equally useful in the right situation, because it too can disrupt your adversary's plans and exploit their weakness when they least expect it. For example, if your adversary is strong and secure, showing no signs of weakness, you prepare yourself for an attack. If she is short-tempered, you should find ways to irritate her. If she is vain, you can accelerate her fatal conceit by pretending to be weak. The Opportunist plays with her adversary like a cat plays with a mouse, first by feigning confusion or weakness and then by pouncing. If your adversary is resting, give her no peace. If your adversary's forces are united, find ways to separate them and disrupt the opportunity for factions to organize.

You must prevent your opponents from drawing you into a zero-sum game, a situation in which your interests and your adversary's are diametrically opposed. This kind of balance is inherently unstable, which means the contest does not end but keeps going until it finds a new equilibrium. As I said in Chapter 4, don't go for the once-and-for-all solution or the instant checkmate. Asserting yourself politically can be exhausting, but you must not let failure or a prolonged stalemate weaken your resolve or distract you from your ultimate goal. The time to be most vigilant is precisely at the moment when your gains and your adversary's are exactly balanced. Prolonged conflict is certain to dampen your enthusiasm and take the edge off your skills.

The importance of self-restraint, of putting limitations on action and inaction, should be clear by now. Haste may bring you luck once in a while, but eventually your luck will run out. When you are on the defensive, haste is particularly disadvantageous. You should calculate your adversary's endurance and factor it into your decision matrix. Power can be the decisive factor in short conflicts (as I said in Archetype 5: the Judo Master) but the longer a conflict lasts the more important endurance becomes. There is no advantage to prolonged conflict, whereas there can be many advantages to well-timed short conflicts. Once you choose to take action, you should do it without any mental reservations.

What are the decisive factors in political conflict when you are emulating (or facing) this archetype? As stated, power is decisive only in short conflicts. Haste can be decisive, especially when it takes the form of audacity (*chutzpah* in Yiddish), but it carries significant risk. Timing is important, and Sun Tzu is very specific about this. Your timing must be slightly ahead of your adversary. Remember to include this variable when you read the field—that is, do not merely calculate the power differential, but also consider, from your adversary's perspective, the range of alternatives and the timing of any movements.

There is something else worth repeating that applies even to this most militaristic archetype. The goal of all political action is to produce the maximum positive outcome while optimizing scarce resources and minimizing waste. Thus, your goal is more complex than total conquest. Your goal should be to break your adversary's resistance without fighting, and without losing sight of all the conditions and constraints that may make your first choice unavailable. Politics is the art of the second-best solution. In some cases, you may be able to produce lasting influence, but in most cases you should measure your success to the extent you have outwitted your adversary by disrupting her foolish plans.

Sun Tzu listed some precise ratios to guide your decision-making, which are politically useful if we dig a little deeper. If your forces are superior at a ratio of 10:1, then you should surround your adversary. If the ratio is 5:1, then you should attack. If the ratio is 2:1, then you should divide your army and attack from the rear or execute a diversionary tactic. Although we are talking about politics rather than war, Sun Tzu's point is pertinent: Know when to fight and when not to fight. Clearly, different ratios call for different tactics, but the power differential is not the only variable. You must also take into consideration the situation, the timing, and all the resources at your disposal. Translation: Superior force is no match for intelligent strategy.

When you do play offense, you will be more successful if you confront your adversary where he or she has not taken adequate precautions. A good example of this is presidential candidate John Kerry, who served honorably in Vietnam. In the 2004 presidential election, Kerry had a clear edge in this regard because the incumbent, George W. Bush, served in the Texas Air National Guard but never in combat. However, because Kerry had a clear edge, he did not think he would have to defend his combat record. This left Kerry totally unprepared and thoroughly overwhelmed by the criticism of his combat record, which became known as "swift-boating" after the name of the political action committee that paid for the advertising.

Undefended places are weak points where you (or your adversary) have not taken adequate precautions. When you are in a defensive position, you must be prepared for anything, even those areas where an attack is unlikely. Your preparations must be so thorough that your adversary will not know where to attack. When you are in a defensive position—to use the principle in reverse—you should attack where it is least expected, which may or may not be your adversary's greatest weakness. By confronting your adversary where and when it is least expected, you force her to defend herself, which means you still have the initiative.

The key to this archetype is not to deny or minimize the danger in any way but to adapt your way of thinking to the situation. This means temporarily, not permanently adapting your thinking. You should master the crisis, take action (or not), be thorough, and not linger any longer than necessary. Once you have climbed the mountain, it is just as important to climb back down. If you grow too accustomed to any crisis, your behavior may become rigid and your response inappropriate once the crisis has passed. (I believe there should be a module in every course on crisis management called *climbing down the mountain*, which means normalizing your response when conditions return to normal after the crisis.)

Any crisis demands respect, but your response should last no longer than the crisis itself. Think of the attacks on the World Trade Center in New York on September 11, 2001. The first phase of the crisis began at 8:45 a.m. when the first plane crashed into the north tower. The second of the two towers fell less than two hours later, which pushed the crisis into a new phase: the formal declaration of a state of emergency, the search for survivors, and the hunt for those responsible. If you look at the timeline of events on the morning of September 11, you see the attacks, from start to finish, lasted less than two hours. The government's response as of this writing, however, has lasted 12 years. When you are in a crisis, it is important not to overact. This is why micropolitics does not encourage you to rely on the false hope that your adversary will not bother you, but teaches preparation—particularly self-mastery and situational awareness—so you will be ready if there is a fight, but not anxious to start one. Of all the political preparations you can make—for offense, for defense, or for doing nothing—the most important of all is to conceal your intentions.

Each of the archetypes is valuable in the right situation, and it is up to you to recognize the right situation. Because micropolitics is fluid, the ability to read the field and the players and then adapt your response appropriately is an essential element of self-mastery. Your goal should not be rote memorization. Of course, it will be helpful to learn how to identify tactics used against you. The next level is the ability to mobilize and utilize tactics on your own behalf. By mastering a variety of tactics instead of relying habitually on one or two, you can win people over not just by threats, intimidation, or coercion, but through your unassuming modesty and sincerity.

You should never publicly share your unconscious or half-conscious thinking, but calculate everything for effect. This is not a mathematical calculation but a political calculation, which has to do with the distribution of power, specifically how your share of the power market increases or decreases. The distribution of power will fluctuate—political coalitions will integrate or disintegrate—in response to other variables in the system. This is the art of the possible. It is important never to allow yourself to feel too secure in your position, especially during a lull in activity and after you have achieved a victory. During the lull, you may well assume that your adversary is setting a trap for you or planning some sort of unpleasant surprise. If you allow yourself to become complacent, you will not learn to exercise power with precision and grace.

Calculating for effect can be tricky because you must remain on the alert for the political tactics of others. Take nothing at face value. By the same token, you should *offer* nothing at face value. Example: the public apology. People who have little or no self-control say and do things unintentionally and apologize later on. What if you knew exactly what you wanted to say or do, and knew that you would apologize for it afterward? In other words, what if you factored your future apology into your calculation? First, this would make apologizing much easier because you will have already accomplished your goal. (By the way, I am talking about *sincerely* apologizing, not *pretending* to apologize.) Second, factoring your apology into your calculation keeps things from getting too ugly, and allows you to be generous and magnanimous. After all, it was none other than Winston Churchill who said we must be resolute in war and defiant in defeat, but also magnanimous in victory.[69] You can afford to be generous when you've accomplished your goal and gotten what you want, after you've climbed the mountain and climbed back down.

Type 8: The Survivor

This eighth and final archetype draws from two major sources. One is *Man's Search for Meaning* by Austrian psychiatrist and Holocaust survivor Viktor Frankl, in which he recounted his experiences as a prisoner in the Auschwitz and Dachau concentration camps. The other source is *Crowds and Power* by Elias Canetti, an epic meditation on the personal, cultural, and collective forces in human nature. Canetti was a man of letters, a Nobel Prize–winning writer and social psychologist who was born in Bulgaria but worked for many years in Britain and Switzerland. There is a long chapter in *Crowds and Power* called "The Survivor," which opens with a bang: "The moment of survival is the moment of power. Horror at the sight of death turns into satisfaction that it is someone else who is dead. The dead man lies on the ground while the survivor stands."[70]

Like Sun Tzu's *Art of War*, Canetti's book overflows with images of warfare and weapons. Here's another example: "The survivor knows of many deaths. If he has been in battle, he has seen those around him fall. He went into battle with the conscious intention of maintaining his ground against the enemy. His declared aim was to dispatch as many of them as possible and he can only conquer if he succeeds."[71] In one gruesome metaphor, Canetti compared interrogation to vivisection (the anatomical dissection of a live animal or human being). Interrogation is forcible intrusion, he wrote, an instrument of power that cuts into your flesh and internal organs like a scalpel. And the interrogator is a special kind of surgeon who doesn't anaesthetize you, but keeps you alive and deliberately inflicts pain so he can learn everything he wants.[72] Reading this, I hope you're convinced that we should communicate (as much as we can) without appropriating the violence and vocabulary of warfare.

Canetti's prose is vivid and bombastic but particularly concise when it comes to this insight: victory and survival, he said, are one and the same. This example of symmetric equality—victory is survival and survival is victory—is important when you remember that politics is the art of the possible. Politics is the art of recognizing when you have only one choice. It's not your first choice or your second, not even your third, but it is a choice nonetheless. If you can survive again and again—even when you have lost everything—you will accumulate "moments of survival" and increase your capacity to face future challenges.

This brings us to Viktor Frankl's search for meaning in the Auschwitz and Dachau concentration camps. It was, he said, "an unrelenting struggle for daily bread and for life itself, for one's own sake or for that of a good friend."[73] Frankl and his fellow prisoners experienced daily and hourly threats of death, lived on a starvation diet, received inadequate medical care, inadequate housing and clothing, and no news from family members who may have been working and suffering under the same cruel conditions or who may have died months ago. As he endured the unendurable—great horrors and relentless little torments—he lost everything except the ability to choose his attitude.

When you live under such extraordinary conditions, when the distribution of power is so inequitable, you must respond accordingly. In Frankl's account—and remember he was also a psychiatrist—he called this response "emotional death" or mortification of normal reactions.[74] Under these terrible conditions, which were constantly dangerous and utterly hopeless, everyone contemplated suicide at one time or another. The most popular method was running into the electrified fence that ran the perimeter of the camp. For Frankl, this was perhaps the first occasion during which he chose his attitude, and he chose to endure the unendurable. According to his calculation, the life expectancy of the average Auschwitz prisoner was very short. Although death could come at any time and in an astonishing variety of ways—execution, starvation, forced labor, illness, and torture—Frankl lost his fear of death because he calculated that running into the electrified fence would actually be worse than the gas chamber. That's all it took for him to decide against suicide.

For me, however, the most moving section of Frankl's book was his description of the role cigarettes played in the life of the camp. Cigarettes were not for smoking, at least not for prisoners without special privileges who did not receive a regular supply. In the camp's micro-economy, you didn't smoke your cigarettes but used them as currency to trade, for an extra soup ration for yourself or your friend, for example. Other than "capos" (the prisoners who performed low-ranking administrative tasks and carried out the most gruesome orders) the only prisoners who smoked their cigarettes were the ones who had lost their will to live. You could recognize them, wrote Frankl, because they stopped saving their cigarettes or trading them. Having lost their will to live, and wanting to enjoy their final moments, they smoked their cigarettes and passed away.

In a way, the Survivor archetype puts micropolitics to the ultimate test because in human history it is impossible to find a situation with a greater power differential than there was between prisoners and guards in a concentration camp. Frankl wrote, "Those who have not gone through a similar experience can hardly conceive of the soul-destroying mental conflict and clashes of will power which a famished man experiences."[75] Yes, precious few of us will go through a similar experience, God willing, but Frankl's experience is a test case as well as a valuable learning tool—that is, if mortification of the emotions leads you to make survival your goal, and to disregard anything that does not serve that goal.

Politics is about power, and mastering this archetype requires regressing to a primitive level. It requires you to separate physical pain from emotional pain, and it requires you to separate how the world is abusing you from how you respond to the abuse. Between any stimulus coming from the environment and your reaction, there is a gap. That gap may be smaller than the head of a pin and shorter than one second, but it is manageable. If you can separate different kinds of pain the way you distinguish different kinds of tension (creative versus emotional) you can manage the gap, the stimulus, and your response.

Frankl drew an analogy to the behavior of gas, which is painful to read but instructive. If you pumped gas into an empty room, it would fill the room completely and uniformly. If the room was not completely empty, the gas would flow around the solid objects, slowly flowing into the empty spaces and all the cracks and crevices. This analogy reveals the key to self-development when you really are surrounded by obstacles, and you really are a prisoner. How do you respond?

First, you should assume it would be impossible to directly over-come any of the obstacles you face. Second, you should assume the obstacles you face are temporary. Based on these two assumptions, the best solution is indirect, and the best use of your time—be-cause the obstacles are temporary—is self-development. It helps to remember Type 4 (the Recluse) and remember how much power the prison exerts over you. But your goal here, unlike the Recluse, isn't a dignified reclusion from politics. Your goal is survival. Do not let the situation defeat you. Do not rush blindly forward and do not struggle because that will make your predicament worse. Turn your back on things for a moment and use the occasion for self-development. Examine your motives, goals, and behavior for clues until the crisis loses its natural momentum. In other words, seek the error within.

Everyone says that if you want to change the world, first you must change yourself. *Be the change you wish to see in the world.* Isn't that what Mahatma Gandhi said? But no one tells you how. You may write off Gandhi's famous dictum as a cliché. But have you considered the alternative? Can you expect to push the problem back onto the people around you? Can you expect people to reject everything you dislike and replace it with everything you support? Managing the gap between stimulus and response means flooding that gap with your self-respect, your moral authority, and the values you cherish most. Every day, politicians scold us, scare us, and make promises they cannot keep. It is hopeless to stake everything on the *Candidate of Hope* because self-mastery does not come from the outside. Expecting your community, your organization, your family to change is futile unless you take personal responsibility. I am not telling you to "become the change" so you can change the world, but so that you—like gas filling every crack and crevice—can assign meaning to your life.

Although micropolitics is not therapy (far from it), Frankl's account of being treated like an animal, and his response to ver-bal abuse and random beatings, is extremely insightful. He was a neurologist and a psychiatrist who wrote with great conviction about the search for meaning. He was a reliable witness to the most unbearable forms of suffering and the cruelest elements of human nature. He was a survivor who denied his consent, rejected the futility of his condition, and found a way to assign meaning to his life. I would like to apply this to our previous definition of individuation: It is the supremely private and uniquely individual act of assigning meaning to your life. The meaning is the "why" of your existence, and the meaning is inseparable from your individual identity. Part of your understanding, therefore, must be future-oriented; that is, realizing that the future still expects something from you. When you have no future preference, no expectation that the future will be better than the past, you stop trading your cigarettes and start smoking them. This devalues your life and robs the future of someone irreplaceable: You.

When people feel pain or go through hard times, first they want to end the suffering, but then they just want to forget about it. Multiply this by a million, and then multiply it again throughout several generations and you get a society that forgets its history, forgets its long journey out of the cave. You get an epidemic of people who have lost the capacity for moral authority, who look to the government (or some other external entity) for their salvation, and eventually they become dependent on society. Forgetting the long shadow that the cave dweller casts over human nature helps perpetuate this disastrous myth, which claims that everything comes to you from the outside, which is the exact opposite of individuation and the entire message of this book. Individuation—the internalization of authority—is what transforms a prisoner into The Survivor, makes you an autonomous agent, and can give meaning to your life.

The specific example Frankl gave to illustrate his point while he was a prisoner is thinking about his beloved wife. Although he did not know whether she was alive or dead, he contemplated her image, communed with her, and even conversed with her because his love fed him and gave him strength. This led Frankl to the following conclusion: The ultimate and highest purpose to which any human can aspire is love. Someone who has lost everything in terms of material wealth and status, who has lost her health and freedom, may still know happiness—no matter how briefly—through contemplation of her loved ones. As Jesus said in his Sermon on the Mount (Matthew 5:44), "Love your enemies, bless them that curse you, do good to them that hate you, and pray for them which despitefully use you, and persecute you." Thus, the Survivor who has lost everything, who has nothing but the power to choose, may still choose love.

Part III

From Apprentice
to Master

Chapter 7

What's It All About?

Don't wait for it to happen; don't even want it to happen. Just watch what does happen.

—Jimmy Malone (Sean Connery) to Eliot Ness (Kevin Costner) in *The Untouchables*

Let's summarize everything up to this point. This book is for people who hate power games, but who also recognize that politics takes place in any kind of organization. There is a mystique to politics, which goes down to the very foundations of human life. This mystique gives special significance to power, the acquisition of power, and the distribution of power. The concept of power is what makes politics different from any other field of human endeavor, and what distinguishes political science from all other social sciences. Without this concept, there would be no need for political science at all. Other fields have their place, their own standards, their own ways of measuring success, but none supersedes the autonomy of the political sphere.

Politics is any social relationship that facilitates control of one human over another. Politics is an interpersonal situation that by definition requires at least two people interacting, taking cues from and responding to one another in an ongoing spiral of give and take. People are by nature political animals and engage in politics because it serves their self-interest. Self-interest is the essence of politics and the most reliable standard to judge political action. Among the different instruments of power, cultural conditioning is the most subtle and most effective.

Leadership, like political behavior in general, is a social behavior requiring at least two participants (or members of a group). The group can be as small as two people, but if one member of the group has influence over another, then one is the leader and the other is the follower. Thus, leadership is always defined by a specific situation and always depends on the response of followers. Our definition must be precise because *leadership is a relationship*. It isn't something you can keep in inventory. It depends on the cue-giving/cue-taking circle to remain unbroken.

Our purpose here is to develop your political imagination and sharpen your political instincts. This includes improving your skill at general pattern recognition and helping you see that few political behaviors, events, or interactions are unprecedented one-of-a-kind situations. If you look closely enough at the details, of course every situation is unique, but the "way out" of the situation is not necessarily in the details. The way out is to use the archetypes—the pre-existent forms and patterns of behavior—to read the field and the players, calculate the power differential, and adapt your response accordingly. The political archetypes represent typical situations and serve to show politics is usually *an instance of* something.

Having read this far, you may feel overwhelmed or reluctant to burden yourself with what appears to be a lifetime of work. However, the path toward self-mastery is trod in small steps. Most of the work is like the "broken window" theory of policing: fixing problems when they are small—repairing broken windows and cleaning up litter to reduce vandalism. The idea is that one broken window sends a signal that nobody cares, and nobody will care about another one.[1] Thus, if you stay on top of small problems and petty crimes, you can prevent a good neighborhood from decaying into a bad one. Likewise, by turning inward and policing your own minor transgressions, you too can prevent decay. This is why I have long respected the somewhat boring profession of dentistry (at least as it is practiced in America), in which dentists are so dedicated to prevention. This is perhaps the closest analogy to micropolitics and self-mastery, which is a way of life involving daily practice and persistence.

I said before that politics is not the exclusive domain of great personalities. At the risk of contradicting myself, I'd like to make one last digression, not to ancient Greece or Hollywood this time, but to Rome and the year AD 161, when Marcus Aurelius became emperor. He reigned honorably and competently (for the most part) for 19 years until his death in 180. Marcus Aurelius was a warrior as well as a statesman, and for several years commanded Rome's armies in the field. At night, however, he was a philosopher, and devoted his time and energy to documenting his *Meditations*, and developed the habit of carving out a little territory for himself where he could distance himself from the confusion and turmoil of the world, and above all be free to *think things through*. (As an aside, I think this qualifies Marcus Aurelius as an introvert, and helps to explain exactly what makes the introvert's guiding orientation so powerful.

When you retire into yourself, none of the tumult and trouble in the world can reach into your soul unless you invite it in.[2])

Marcus Aurelius received early training in the doctrine of Stoicism, which included, among other things, dressing plainly and living simply. The Stoics also believed in thinking logically, behaving ethically, and exercising self-control, all of which are elements of micropolitics. In the modern era, stoicism has become synonymous with stubborn endurance, resistance to hardship, and persistence in the midst of adversity. For me, persistence in the midst of adversity means staying power, and it's a very potent force. Do you remember from Chapter 1 the difference between seduction and courtship? The difference is persistence—this doesn't mean staying in one location or staying with one organization for a lifetime. Staying power begins with an idea (which typifies introversion as a guiding orientation), and then making a commitment to that idea, literally making a promise and doing your best to keep it.

Permit me to share an example from my own life. When I joined the Peace Corps in 1982, my assignment was to build a primary school in a small village in southeastern Gabon. I had a crew of six villagers, and we communicated in French. We made cinder blocks by hand and dried them in the sun. We had no running water. We had no electricity, which meant no power tools. But we had one of those old-style Toyota pickup trucks, a boom box, and a few well-worn cassette tapes, which I inherited from another volunteer who had recently completed his service. One morning, I connected the boom box to the truck battery, popped in the Temptations Greatest Hits, and played "Papa Was a Rollin' Stone." My workers started dancing and I started dancing. It was a moment of cross-cultural exchange. That experience—not just that moment but the whole Peace Corps experience, living in another country, immersed in another culture—was so profound, so intense, it made everything else seem unworthy by comparison. Well, that morning I had an epiphany. I decided then and there that whatever else I did with my life, my education, and my career, it would be international. That's the promise I made to myself.

This may seem like an easy promise to keep (fancy hotels and exotic locations) but there have been times that tested me. Those tests were opportunities for reflection, but they were also challenging, exasperating, and sometimes heartbreaking. A few weeks after I completed my Peace Corps service in Gabon, I moved to Burundi (in East Africa) where I worked for the American embassy and the Agency for International Development on a famine relief project. A few weeks after I arrived in Burundi, I received a telegram from home. My father had died. I knew he was ill, so the news was not unexpected, but it was devastating nonetheless. I flew home to California for the memorial service in a state of shock. I felt a terrible loss but also guilty about being so far from home when he died.

After Burundi, I spent five months traveling around the world with extended stops in several countries in East Africa and Asia. The highlight was six weeks in Nepal, which included trekking north of Kathmandu in the Langtang Valley up to Kyanjin Gompa, a little village near the Tibetan border. When I returned to the United States, the best job I could find was selling vacuum cleaners. My father had worked in the "floorcare industry," as they call it, after he emigrated from England to America in 1948. He got his start in the business working for Hoover selling door to door. Just before he died, my father had started a new job with a new company; when I got home, the company president offered me a job too. I was married and needed the money, so I accepted the offer to manage the company's Northern California territory. Determined to keep that international promise to myself, I also enrolled in the master's program in international business at San Francisco State University.

When the company decided to enter the European market, the company president asked me to launch its European subsidiary. While still working in Northern California, I traveled back and forth between San Francisco and Europe doing market research and developing a strategic plan. In spring 1989, I relocated to Germany, launched the company there, and started making appointments with buyers at department stores, discount chain stores, distributors, and anyone else who would hear my sales pitch.

Shortly after I arrived in Europe, I received more bad news. My mother suffered a stroke. Her condition was not life-threatening, but she was completely paralyzed on one side of her body. This time, I was determined not to repeat my mistake. I decided there were more important things than keeping that promise I made to myself (at least in the short-term) and immediately started planning my exit strategy: As soon as the subsidiary was up and running, which I estimated would take a year, I would return to California.

In retrospect, this may seem like another easy decision, but it was an incredibly exciting time to be in Germany. Having the good fortune and good timing to be in Germany in November 1989 when the Berlin Wall fell symbolized everything I loved about international affairs. It was like having the same epiphany all over again. To top it off, Germany won the World Cup in the summer of 1990, and the celebration that followed gave new meaning to the phrase "all-nighter." The two Germanys reunified that October, and one week later, I found myself back in California. I bought a condominium close to the house where I grew up and not far from the nursing home where my mother was living. She passed away eight months later.

I returned to San Francisco State to complete my master's degree and teach in the Department of International Business. After I graduated, I began the doctoral program at the University of Hawaii. While working on my dissertation, I took a job in Bulgaria, where I managed an economic development project to facilitate Bulgaria's transition to a market economy. Then I returned to Hawaii to finish writing my doctoral dissertation. A few weeks after I received my degree, I started losing weight—a lot of weight. I was thirsty all the time and urinating frequently, going 10 to 15 times a day. It took the doctor a few seconds to make the diagnosis: diabetes. Does it run in the family? Yes, on my mother's side. Long story short: three injections of insulin per day, every day, starting immediately. I was 36 years old and otherwise perfectly healthy. That was 17 years ago, which means I have given myself more than 17,000 shots since then.

The daily injections took some getting used to at first, but eventually became part of my daily routine, like shaving or brushing my teeth. At the time, however, what really bugged me was not getting to enjoy my academic success very long. I know being diagnosed with a chronic illness isn't the same as losing a parent, but it spoiled what should have been a moment of triumph, and forced me to retreat into that little territory, as Marcus Aurelius called it. Stubborn endurance was the only option.

I could go on but I think you get the general idea. There is an old adage attributed to Socrates: "The unexamined life is not worth living." To me, the word *unexamined* means untested, and the untested life is not worth living. The way you test your life is by asserting your power—not by making an ostentatious display of force, but through persistence, which is humble, gentle, and inconspicuous. In the section about Archetype 3: the Mentor, I mentioned the gentle breeze that blows along the coast in San Francisco's Golden Gate Park. Most of the time, the wind does not blow very strongly, but it blows consistently in the same direction and sculpts and twists the trees into the most fascinating forms. This is proof of staying power, which may be the most powerful force in the universe. Staying power is influence that never lapses. This kind of power is gradual and inconspicuous, but durable, and thus, easy to underestimate.

And this is what micropolitics is all about: how you respond to adversity. Most likely, you will never experience anything like what Viktor Frankl went through as a concentration camp prisoner. However, you will certainly have adversity in your life. Let me repeat something from Chapter 4. Your long-term, habitual response to adversity is an important indicator of your self-mastery. This is not to minimize the immediate psychological shock of any traumatic event, but to emphasize what happens after the shock has worn off. If you can remain composed while others are paralyzed by fear and trembling, that's a sign of self-mastery. You should not back away from adversity because—depending on your response—adversity can build capacity and serve as the foundation of future success.

The Foundation of Freedom

If you listen to talk radio as I do, you often hear that government is too big, too costly, and too intrusive in our daily lives. If you listen to conservative talk radio, you hear the solution is to cut taxes, shrink the size of government, starve it, and weaken it. What if you agree with the problem but disagree with the solution? What if you dislike big government (and big business, big religion, and big education) with equal intensity, but seek a solution that is more personal, less ideological, and less grandiose? If so, micropolitics provides an alternative to the modern state's concentration of power.

If that sentence makes you jump from your chair and shout "I knew it!" you may now return to your seat. This is not a conservative manifesto extolling the virtues of limited government, even though I believe the modern state breeds dependency among the beneficiaries and a relentless self-deception among the benefactors who cannot see the harm they are doing. Thus, it must be said that micropolitics is the antidote to many of the social ills the modern state attempts to cure. In that sense, micropolitics and traditional politics are competitors, except there is little potential for governmental overreach and the abuse of power with micropolitics because of the emphasis on self-mastery.

"In the last analysis," wrote Jung, "the essential thing is the life of the individual."[3] When you read *the essential thing is the life of the individual*, does it make you think twice? If so, that's because (as I said in Chapter 1) any understanding of micropolitics based entirely on the individual would be incomplete. Our understanding of politics begins with the individual, but then ventures toward all points on the compass, outward because a political animal is a social animal, and downward because of the cultural and collective forces at work, but also inward, toward your identifications, demands, and expectations. As a reminder, your identifications are the categories to which you belong, your demands are your desired outcomes, and your expectations are your beliefs about the future, particularly your expectations that the future will be *better* than the past. If you have no future preference—no expectation that the future will be better than the past—it devalues your life and robs the future of someone irreplaceable.

Unfortunately, your expectations about the future will have no effect on your distaste for politics. If you find politics inherently distasteful, clearly you will have overcome it (or at least learn to live with it). It may help to remember that political behavior is an essential element of human nature. Even if you choose to abstain from it, you should remember that whenever there are two or more people in a room (or a cave or a spacecraft), chances are that one of them will introduce power and thus politicize the situation. Even if you choose never to play offense, that does not mean you should not play a little defense, and it certainly does not mean you have to surrender. Regardless, you should never deceive yourself that other people, especially those who *claim* to share your distaste for politics, are not sharpening their knives for you.

As stated, I have been studying political phenomena a long time, and have observed certain recurring patterns, situations, and participants. Politics has a reputation as some sort of exaggerated or corrupted version of normal society and skilled political practitioners have the status of outlaws. Is politics as bad as people say? Regardless of its reputation, I consider politics an effective instrument of progress. Politics is society's method for the distribution of power and resources. Politics is the way you and I preserve our freedom and how future generations will preserve theirs. Politics is not poisonous unless you permit it to be. One way you can permit it is by becoming a host organism for the kind of toxic politics that benefits no one, a kind of human incubator that feeds and shelters toxic politics, and enables it to reproduce without even knowing it. Then you and everyone around you become political prisoners, never charged, never convicted, but effectively held captive nonetheless.

As Frankl said, "If there is a meaning in life at all, then there must be a meaning in suffering. Suffering is an ineradicable part of life, even as fate and death. Without suffering and death human life cannot be complete."[4] Sadly, Frankl's account of life in a concentration camp was not the last horrifying example of suffering and death. Since WWII, there have been numerous instances of mass murder—not on the scale of the Holocaust, but shocking nonetheless. At least 500,000 and as many as 3 million people died in Bangladesh in 1971; 1.7 million people in Cambodia in 1975–79; hundreds of thousands in Bosnia in 1992–95; 800,000 in Rwanda in 1994; and tens of thousands in Darfur, Sudan, since 2004. These are instances in which the power differential is so extreme that it makes everything I have written here inadequate by comparison. Nonetheless, Frankl's personal experiences in Auschwitz and Dachau, plus his personal observations of prisoners comforting their fellow prisoners, demonstrates that people always have a choice. The many small gestures Frankl witnessed—prisoners nursing the sick or giving away their last piece of bread—are proof that even under the extreme emotional and physical conditions of a Nazi concentration camp, you can still preserve your spiritual freedom and your independence of mind. Even when you have lost everything else, you have not lost the ability to choose your attitude. The sort of person any individual becomes—that means you and me—is not the result of environmental forces but of individual choice.

My point is to remind you where the foundation of freedom is located. Never forget that you are the life-carrier. Not the culture, not the collective, and certainly not the government; you are the life-carrier.[5] "A living man can be enslaved and reduced to the historic condition of an object," wrote Camus, "but if he dies in refusing to be enslaved, he reaffirms the existence of another kind of human nature which refuses to be classified as an object."[6] I disagree with the part about reaffirming another *kind* of human nature but would say the act of resistance reveals and reaffirms an essential element of human nature. You can play the role assigned to you—a role of infinitesimal significance not much different than a slave—or you can play a role that you assign for yourself. You should not let yourself become a function of society. You should not permit yourself to become a "human resource" to be plugged into (or cruelly unplugged from) the labor market. This is the foundation of freedom for you and everyone around you.

Forgive me if this is repetitious, but micropolitics is a gentle art, which is assertive without being aggressive. As your self-mastery increases, so will your self-respect and self-confidence. This will radiate outward and change the way people perceive you. Additionally, it will increase your ability to influence the behavior of the people around you: subordinates and superiors, and of course your peers. Authentic leadership never comes from the corner office in any organization because there is nothing in an organization's hierarchy or division of labor that guarantees leadership. Once you have achieved a certain level of competence, you will increase your expectations and naturally redirect your goals. As your competence increases, so will your expectations and the difficulty factor of the goals you set. The paradox is that your batting average—a performance indicator equally reliable for baseball hitters and cricket batsmen—will probably drop. The important thing is not to lose sight of your goal, not to compromise your integrity, and never to forget your promises.

In closing, I would like to quote the immortal Dicky Fox, the Original Sports Agent from the film *Jerry Maguire*. (If you're keeping track, Dicky Fox would be an example of Type 3: the Mentor.) Dicky said, "Hey, I don't have all the answers. In life, to be honest, I failed as much as I have succeeded. But I love my wife. I love my life. And I wish you my kind of success." In micropolitics, success means knowing the purpose and goal of your life and proceeding humbly toward that goal. I wish you that kind of success.

Appendix

On Bullying

In this Appendix, I want to draw your attention to something I said about making political triage your top priority. You have a duty on a battlefield or in an emergency room to treat the sickest people first, treat as many as possible, and still take care of yourself. And this brings me to the point: This book is about self-mastery, self-discipline, self-development, and self-defense. But this Appendix is about self-sacrifice.

In this context, self-sacrifice means ignoring your political goals, denying your self-interest, and putting yourself at risk on behalf of someone else. I'm not suggesting human nature has taken a holiday or that the laws of politics are any less relentless than before. I am suggesting that your mastery of micropolitics implies a duty to help the people around you—your subordinates, your peers, and your superiors. I am suggesting that you use the tools and techniques in this book to prevent bullying, the same way Captain America uses that distinctive shield of his. This is a good reminder that micropolitics doesn't use offensive weapons, but relies entirely on defensive and nonviolent tools and techniques.

What is bullying? According to StopBullying.gov, a Website managed by the U.S. Department of Health and Human Services, "Bullying is unwanted, aggressive behavior among school-aged children that involves a real or perceived power imbalance. The behavior is repeated, or has the potential to be repeated, over time. Bullying includes actions such as making threats, spreading rumors, attacking someone physically or verbally, and excluding someone from a group on purpose."[1]

Three things leap out. First is the "real or perceived power imbalance." When I say politics is about power, the acquisition of power, the distribution of power, and the uses and abuses of power, this is what I mean. Second, this definition is mainly concerned with children who are victims of other children, but when I say the laws of politics are rooted in human nature, this goes for children too. Third, bullying may be physical or verbal, and this holds true for workplace bullying. In the schoolyard or the workplace, an imbalance of power may be created by differences in size and physical strength, popularity, or cognitive ability. But in the workplace, an imbalance of power may also be created by differences in rank on the organizational chart. As I said early on, power is anything that facilitates control of one human over another. Any imbalance of power (real or perceived) facilitates the bully's control.

The idea of using the tools and techniques of micropolitics to prevent bullying occurred to me fairly recently, when a colleague gave me three anti-bullying signs. These signs were printed on heavy stock paper, in different colors, and were obviously meant to be posted. One was titled *Are You a Workplace Bully?* Below the title was a checklist describing the common characteristics of a workplace bully and a message encouraging the reader to check all that apply. The characteristics: charming, seductive, dominating, hypocritical, evasive, self-righteous, and passive-aggressive. To this list, I would add *cowardly*—but it doesn't matter because most bullies are never going to read it. And if they did, for them it would be like looking into a magic mirror that distorts reality, making the bully look good and the victim look bad.

The second anti-bullying sign was titled *Been Targeted by a Bully at Work?* Below the title was a list of tactics that bullies commonly use.[2] These tactics include making false accusations, staring or glaring, and social isolation (giving the silent treatment, keeping someone "out of the loop," or encouraging coworkers to turn against the victim). Other tactics include making up new and/or arbitrary rules that don't apply to the bully, discrediting the quality or quantity of the victim's work, spreading rumors, failing to stop rumors, throwing temper tantrums, retaliating against victims after they have complained, taking credit for someone else's work, and using the performance evaluation process to undermine the victim. The list goes on. Taken together, these tactics are nothing less than a systematic abuse of power.

The third anti-bullying sign was titled *Have You Witnessed Bullying at Work and Done Nothing?* This is the one that got to me. And now I am asking you: Have you ever witnessed bullying and done nothing? Why? Did you think stopping it was someone else's responsibility? Were you confused because the situation seemed unclear? Did you decide not to intervene because nobody else intervened? When you saw and heard what was happening, were you frightened? Did this trigger your survival instinct? Did you think the next victim might be you? Did you calculate the cost/benefit ratio and simply decide to take sides with the bully?

I remember the first time I read this sign. I felt ashamed of myself. I started trying to remember if I had witnessed any of the tactics, the systematic abuse of power, and did nothing to intervene. But I also felt angry. I wondered why I did not stand up and say, *Hitherto shalt thou come, but no farther.*[3] Not many people speak the English of King James anymore, I'll admit; why not simply say *that's far enough.*

Let me make a suggestion: Please rent or buy a copy of *Pulp Fiction*, Quentin Tarantino's 1994 masterpiece, and watch Samuel L. Jackson's mangled recitation of Ezekiel 38:17. Jackson's character, Jules, claims to have memorized the verse, but this is pulp fiction. Just listen to the character go on about the tyranny of evil men, the inequities of the selfish, and the Lord's furious anger, and then you will have some idea of how I felt reading this sign for the first time.

What gives you the right to intervene? The answer is Liberation Ethics, which (like micropolitics) is nonviolent and implies the willingness to suffer for others and the unwillingness to inflict suffering.[4] Political scientist and nonviolent activist John Swomley developed liberation ethics in the early 1970s. As a Christian pacifist, Swomley was influenced by Jesus, as well as Mahatma Gandhi and Martin Luther King Jr., all of whom renounced violence. Swomley's liberation ethics begins by debunking three obsolete myths. First is the retaliation myth: your goal is *not* to give your adversaries a taste of their own medicine. Second is the zero-sum myth: your freedom does *not* come at your adversary's expense. Third is the fire-with-fire myth: you must *not* use the methods—including violent methods—that your adversary uses. As Raghavan Iver said in his description of the Servant-Leader, she must be a moral educator who identifies herself with the dreams, activities, and sufferings of the people.[5]

Where does that leave you? *Have you witnessed bullying and done nothing?* Would you like a better answer to this question? If you have read this far, the answer must be yes. First, model the virtues you hope others would emulate, especially emotional self-control and professional detachment, which will help you avoid excessive use of force. Second, talk about bullying and encourage others to do so. We need to create a culture in which people (at least) aren't afraid to talk about bullying. Finally, when you see it, stop it. Don't assume someone else will stop it. Make it your duty. Stand up and say *that's enough*. Repeat after me: *That's far enough*.

Glossary

abstraction: A mental process of separation and removal, which allows you to generalize and categorize your thinking based on a specific instance. The process of abstraction begins with a specific real-world problem and then progresses from the specific to the general. By excluding information and factoring out the details of a specific instance, you can simplify reality and thus make it manageable.

archetype: A model. An archetype is a symbolic formula, which consists of personal, cultural, and collective elements, and represents the preexistent forms and patterns of instinctual behavior common among humans. Archetypes are abstractions and thus resistant to understanding on a purely intellectual level, but emotionally and aesthetically appealing (in terms of sight, touch, sound, color, or texture). Jung derived this concept from his extensive reading of myths, fairy tales, and world literature, and from his practice as a clinical psychologist.

Archimedean point: The imaginary point of view where you (the scholar and/or practitioner of politics) could stand if you wanted perfect objectivity uncorrupted by cultural or emotional influences. It was Greek mathematician Archimedes who claimed he could move the earth if he had a big enough lever and a place to stand.

bureaucratic authority: Ex officio power, meaning power by virtue of position, status, office, wealth, or family ties.

collective element: The primitive, instinctive, and sometimes aggressive characteristic of the political animal. The collective element is shared by all humanity and connects all humanity. While the personal and cultural elements are acquired (and sometimes unacquired), the collective element is hardwired into the species.

compensatory power: The ability to alter someone's behavior by offering (or promising) a reward. Public recognition, office, title, and money (or other valuables) are examples of effective instruments to alter someone's behavior.

complex system: A network of mutuality consisting of an infinite number of systems within subsystems with no floor or ceiling. The elements of a system are interconnected in such a way that changes in one element produce changes elsewhere in the system. Complex systems consist of systems within systems, with multiple decision nodes and decentralized power. Complex systems have the ability to produce results different from the results of individual, unconnected elements and also have the ability to alter the environment in which they function. Complex systems have a relatively low entropy value, meaning the degree of disorder (or anarchy) is below the maximum.

complexity: A set of principles to which systems consistently adhere. This consistency of adherence both permits and promotes interdependence with other systems. This consistency also permits and promotes emergent behavior—that is, behavior beyond a system's former capacity and beyond the capacity of the elemental subsystems. (*See also* complex system.)

condign power: The ability to alter someone's behavior by punishing her. In addition, condign power is the ability to force someone's submission via threat, intimidation, or coercion; for example, by offering a sufficiently unpleasant alternative with adverse consequences.

conditioned power: The ability to alter someone's behavior by changing (literally conditioning) their belief system through persuasion or education. Conditioned power is distinct from condign or compensatory power because the subject may or may not make a conscious choice to accept the reward or avoid the punishment. Conditioned power is subtly effective for perpetuating religious doctrine, winning submission to military policy, and extolling the virtues of fascism, socialism, capitalism, and every other system of political economy.

consigliere: Adviser or counselor. Although the term has negative connotations because of its association with organized crime, many business leaders, professional athletes, entertainers, and especially politicians rely on the services of a consigliere to help manage their companies, their careers, or their political campaigns. (*See* Type 3: the Mentor.)

cultural conditioning: The process of acquiring (and un-acquiring) values and beliefs that influence your behavior. Cultural conditioning is the slow, relentless process that trains people to act in ways or respond in ways "approved" by society.

culture: A set of attitudes, values, and behaviors shared by a community, which are passed from generation to generation, and which are based on trial-and-error learning. (*See also* cultural conditioning.)

extrovert: A political type referring to an individual's sense of objectivity. Generally speaking, the extrovert's sense of objectivity implies a basic orientation toward the external environment. Extroverts are influenced by their external surroundings and oriented by their experience, as opposed to introverts, who are influenced by their inner selves and oriented by their own ideas and principles. (*See also* introvert.)

evolution: A kind of emergent behavior in complex systems that increases a system's behavioral repertoire and relative autonomy, and produces greater capacity for self-reflection and consciousness. Evolutionary change is indicated by increasing diversity, complexity, and organization. In addition, evolution is distinct from ordinary change because it is directional and irreversible.

individuation: The internalization of authority. The ultimate goal of micropolitics: to become a self-determining agent guided by your own principles instead of the commands and principles of others. This includes a holistic sense of objectivity (which integrates introverted [subject-oriented] and extroverted [object-oriented] thinking) and the ability to differentiate between yourself and the cultural and collective elements of the group.

interest: Interest is the essence of politics. Interest is the most reliable standard to judge political action. Interest is synonymous with *special interest*, meaning a specific privilege or financial benefit. An interest is a stake, as in stakeholder with an investment or an interest in a project or organization, who can influence *or be influenced by* the project or organization's activities. In politics, interests and special interest groups (stakes and stakeholders) are inseparable.

introvert: A political type referring to an individual's sense of objectivity. Generally speaking, the introvert's sense of objectivity implies a basic orientation toward his or her own thought processes and emphasizes deference to symbols and a set of inner laws. Introverts are influenced by their inner selves and oriented by their own ideas and principles, as opposed to extroverts who are influenced by their external surroundings and oriented by their experience. (*See also* extrovert.)

leadership: A specific social or interpersonal situation in which someone responds favorably and voluntarily to a leadership cue. Leadership is always defined by a specific situation and realized in the response of followers. If followers respond favorably and voluntarily, there is leadership. If followers do not respond favorably and voluntarily, there is no leadership. No exceptions. (See also *The Symbolic Uses of Politics* by Murray Edelman.)

objectivity: See sense of objectivity.

persona: A persona is a social façade, a kind of mask or camouflage, which you develop based on your experience observing the effect you have on the world. Your persona is not how you actually are, but how you appear to yourself and to the world. Your persona may conceal your motives and interests, and mislead your adversaries and even your friends and allies.

political mystique: A mystique is a social artifact that gives special significance to or casts a false glamour over otherwise ordinary objects and people. The political mystique gives special significance to power, the acquisition of power, and the distribution of power.

politics: Any social (interpersonal) situation in which power is introduced. The essence of politics is self-interest, which is the most reliable standard to judge political action.

power: Power is anything that facilitates control of one human over another. Power is the concept that distinguishes political science from all other social sciences. Power is the medium of exchange in any political situation. Social situations are politicized when power is introduced. (*See also* compensatory power *and* condign power.)

realism (political realism): The ultimate laws of politics, which are rooted in human nature. The main concept of political realism is that politics is about power. This concept is what distinguishes political science from all other social sciences. Without the concept that politics is about power—the acquisition of power, the distribution of power, the uses and abuses of power—there would be no need for political science. Other social sciences have their place, their own standards, their own ways of measuring success, but none supersedes the autonomy of the political sphere.

sanctioned expectation: A belief about the future, specifically the belief that you will maximize (or at least optimize) your self-interest by altering your behavior in response to threats of punishment or promises of reward. When a social situation has been politicized by the introduction of power, the sanctioned expectation is the belief that you will exchange certain behavior (avoidance or acceptance) in response to condign or compensatory power.

sense of objectivity: An individual's guiding orientation toward the external environment or toward his or her own thought processes. There is a spectrum of objectivity with two types (the introvert and the extrovert) at either end. Generally speaking, the extrovert's sense of objectivity implies a basic orientation toward the external environment, while the introvert's implies a basic orientation toward his or her own thought processes and emphasizes deference to symbols and a set of inner laws. Your sense of objectivity affects the way you learn, communicate with the environment, send and receive signals, and classify information, and thus subtly dominates your political imagination.

situational awareness: A skill belonging to high self-monitors who create, cultivate, and project a persona that accounts for the goals and expectations of other people. In micropolitics, situational awareness includes reading the field, reading the players (assessing the strengths and weaknesses of all participants in the situation), calculating the power differential, anticipating the future situation, and adapting your response accordingly.

symbol: Something visible and/or tangible (such as a flag, uniform, or trademark) that represents something abstract. A symbol projects something intangible and larger than itself, which gives it a dual character—partly real and partly unreal—and may communicate what people want or fear, or what they believe is possible. A symbol must have an aesthetic value (in terms of sight, touch, sound, color, or texture) that is emotionally appealing and worthy of our attention, but resistant to understanding on a purely intellectual level.

symbolic formula: *See* archetype.

tension of opposites: A process of change based on the principle of differentiation and inner polarity (the divergence and convergence of opposing forces) within a complex system; an equilibrating process in which opposing forces and competing influences are cancelled out and systems are brought into balance. All systems depend on this inner polarity, without which they could not function.

theory-in-use: Your hypothesis tested against observable data and your standards of success. Your theory-in-use consists of your values, strategies, and assumptions. This is distinct from your "espoused theory," which you use merely to justify or explain your actions. Your theory-in-use actually governs your actions, while your espoused theory is the one you announce publicly.

type: A general tentative classification based on an individual's sense of objectivity (extroverted or introverted). This classification does not refer to psychological or emotional types, but political types that transcend other demographic categories such as education, gender, class, and culture. (*See also* archetype.)

Notes

Preface

1. Hillman, *Kinds of Power*, p. 7.

2. David G. Winter, in Guinote and Vescio, *The Social Psychology of Power*, p. 113.

3. Robert O. Schulze, "The Bifurcation of Power in a Satellite City," in Janowitz, *Community Political Systems*, p. 19.

4. Rosinski, *Power and Human Destiny*, pp. 13–14.

5. Ibid., p. 191.

6. King, *On Writing*, pp. 145–146.

7. Dingwell, "Language, Law, and Power."

8. For a salty assessment of our sexist language, see Ethel Strainchamps in Gornick and Moran, *Woman in Sexist Society*, pp. 347–361.

Chapter 1

1. Karl Loewenstein refers to this mystique as the "demonology of power." Loewenstein, *Political Power*, p. 8.

2. Without power there would be no progress, but progress is distinct from evolution. See Becker, *Progress and Power*, pp. 24–25.

3. See Lasswell, *Power and Personality*, p. 10. Pierre Bourdieu also refers to political space (see Bourdieu, *Distinction*, pp. 451–453), but Bourdieu's space isn't interpersonal the way I define it, following Lasswell's definition of power as an interpersonal situation. Bourdieu's space is closer to the "power market" I mentioned in which individuals and institutions are all categorized and classified, and all exchange "political products" in competition with one another.

4. O'Neill with Novak, *Man of the House*.

5. Lasswell referred to student-practitioners as participant-observers "who give no clue that they are studying anybody for any purpose whatsoever" but who cannot help but influence and be influenced by people. See Lasswell, *The Analysis of Political Behavior*, p. 102.

6. See Calhoun, Li Puma, and Postone, *Bourdieu*, p. 6, and Bailey, *Stratagems and Spoils*, p. 16.

7. Personal correspondence with the author, July 8, 2011.

8. See Lenski, *Power and Privilege*, p. 38.

9. Covey, *The 7 Habits of Highly Effective People*, p. 72.

10. Jennifer R. Overbeck, in Guinote and Vescio, *The Social Psychology of Power*, p. 28. See also Wartenberg, *The Forms of Power*, p. 5; Boulding, *Three Faces of Power*, p. 52; Russell, *Power: A New Social Analysis*, p. 35.

11. Block, *The Empowered Manager*, pp. 11–14.

12. Swingle, *The Management of Power*, pp. 13–14.

13. The methodology used here is what Scottish sociologist Robert MacIver might have characterized as "imaginative reconstruction." See MacIver, *On Community*, p. 263.

14. "Creative politics does not differ from creative science [which] begins where the mind moves away from established patterns; the scientist freely invents tools that do not yet exist as such in nature, although in principle they are based on nature." Karl Mannheim, *Freedom, Power, and Democratic Planning*, p. 30.

Chapter 2

1. Robert Strausz-Hupé put it this way: "All we know with some certainty...is that love of power is a part of human nature." See Strausz-Hupé, *Power and Community*, p. 30.

2. Morgenthau, *Politics Among Nations*, pp. 4–17.

3. According to Harold Lasswell, political science "is the study of influence and the influential" (Lasswell, *Who Gets What*, p. 13). If Lasswell were slightly more precise and said political science is the study of power and the powerful, then I would agree.

4. This is close to Robert Dahl's definition of power, which depicts a political relationship, meaning one individual

had the capacity to act in such a way as to control another individual's responses. See Dahl, *A Preface to Democratic Theory*, p. 13. Floyd Hunter listed several "postulates on power" he considered self-evident; for example, power involves relationships between individuals and groups; power is structured socially; and power is a relatively constant factor in social relationships. See Hunter, *Community Power Structure*, p. 7.

5. "Anyone who hopes that in time it may be possible to abolish war should give serious thought to the problem of satisfying harmlessly the instincts that we inherit from long generations of savages." Russell, *Authority and the Individual*, p. 8.

6. Lasswell, *Power and Personality*, 11–13.

7. Weber, *The Theory of Social and Economic Organization*, p. 152.

8. Burns, *Leadership*, p. 15 (italics original).

9. Strausz–Hupé, *Power and Community*, p. 12.

10. Ibid., p. 4.

11. Fromm, in Maslow, *New Knowledge*, p. 152.

12. See Rubinoff, *The Pornography of Power*, pp. 7–9.

13. Chancer, *Sadomasochism in Everyday Life*, p. 15.

14. See James March in Easton, *Varieties of Power*, p. 68.

15. Plato, *The Republic*, Book VII.

16. See Ascher and Hirschfelder–Ascher, *Revitalizing Political Psychology*, p. 50.

17. Jung, *Psychological Types*, p. 311.

18. Ibid., pp. 324–325.

19. Ellis, *Founding Brothers*, p. 131.

20. According to Chris Argyris, this is your "private world" because every experience is colored by your self–image and your very own set of "personality-determined glasses." Sees Argyris, *Personality and Organization*, pp. 47, 240.

21. Lincoln, Abraham, "Special Message to Congress, July 4, 1861," *Selected Speeches and Writings*. New York: Library of America, 1992: 307 (italics original).

22. Aristotle, *Politics*, Book 5, Chapter IX.

23. Plato, *Republic*, Book 5.

24. Plato, *Republic*, Book 6.

25. Mills, *Power, Politics and People*, p. 310.

26. Duke, *Conflict and Power*, p. 240.

27. Pierre Bourdieu refers to this as *self-exploitation*, which is especially common among mid-level managers who are wage earners subject to strong hierarchical authority and held accountable as independent proprietors. See Bourdieu, *Acts of Resistance*, p. 97. Elizabeth Janeway refers to this exchange as "the abdication of power by the weak." See Janeway, *Powers of the Weak*, p. 159.

28. Jung, *Two Essays*, p. 143.

29. Lipsey and Lancaster, "The General Theory of Second Best," pp. 11–32.

30. Argyris and Schön, *Organizational Learning II*, pp.: 14–15. See also Argyris and Schön, *Organization Learning*, pp. 10–11. According to David Easton, you can infer the "operating values" of participants in a political system (as opposed to operating ideals) by their behavior, which makes articulation unnecessary. See Easton, *A Systems Analysis of Political Life*, p. 290.

31. Argyris and Schön, *Organizational Learning II*, p. 29.

32. Brislin, *The Art of Getting Things Done*, pp. 77–85.

33. Endsley, "Toward a Theory of Situation Awareness," p. 36.

34. Watts, *Power in Family Discourse*, pp.: 54–56, 248.

35. See Greenstein, *Personality and Politics*, pp. 42–45. Greenstein developed this three-part framework for a very different purpose: to emphasize the *limited* capacity of individuals to shape political events. See also Duke, *Conflict and Power*, p. 206.

36. Francis Flynn, in Guinote and Vescio, *The Social Psychology of Power*, p. 288.

37. Ascher and Hirschfelder-Ascher, *Revitalizing Political Psychology*, p. 44.

38. Jung, *Two Essays*, p. 5.

Chapter 3

1. Loewenstein, *Political Power*, pp. 3–18.

2. See Mann, *The Sources of Power, Volume I*, p. 14.

3. Friedan, *The Feminine Mystique*, p. 43.

4. Carol Hanisch, in Sarachild, *Feminist Revolution*, pp. 204–205. In an unpublished manuscript (2006), Hanisch wrote a new introduction in which she divulged that the idea for the title was not hers; she gave credit to the editors of the anthology. In addition, sociologist Sallie Westwood writes, "The personal becomes the political within the complex of practices and discourses that constitute the field of fertility treatment programmes." It is impossible to disagree with this statement. As stated, any social situation becomes political when power is introduced. See Westwood, *Power and the Social*, p. 78.

5. See Lasswell, *Power and Personality*, p. 17.

6. Argyris and Schön, *Organizational Learning II*, p. 8.

7. Argyris and Schön, *Organization Learning*, p. 328. According to Bertrand Russell, "The strongest and most instinctively compelling of social groups was, and still is, the family." See Russell, *Authority and the Individual*, p. 3.

8. Bourdieu, *Distinction*, p. 109.

9. Jennifer R. Overbeck, in Guinote and Vescio, *The Social Psychology of Power*, p. 28. David Winter makes a similar distinction (p. 133).

10. Galbraith, *Anatomy of Power*, pp. 4–6. See also Easton, *A Systems Analysis*, pp. 207–209.

11. Mills, *The Power Elite*.

12. Clegg, *Power, Rule and Domination*, pp. 23–24.

13. Berle, *Power*, pp. 37, 62–67.

14. James Madison considered French political theorist Baron De Montesquieu the ultimate authority on the concept of separation of powers (Federalist No. 47) and likened Montesquieu's contribution to political science to William Shakespeare's contribution to poetry.

15. Kornhauser, *Problems of Power*, p. 189.

16. Galbraith, *Anatomy of Power*, p. 32.

17. Frederick, *Values, Nature, and Culture*, pp. 82–84. Frederick credits Leslie A. White, *The Science of Culture: A Study of Man and Civilization*, New York: Grove Press, 1949.

18. Peace Corps, *Culture Matters*, p. 75.

19. Bourdieu, *Distinction*, p. 175.

20. Friedan, *The Feminine Mystique*, pp. 305–306.

21. Elgin, *The Gentle Art of Verbal Self-Defense*, pp. 264–265. Investigative journalist Lucy Komisar came to the same conclusion. "Social conditioning began in childhood when

fathers went out to work and mothers stayed home, images perpetuated in schoolbooks and games on television." Komisar in Hendel, *The Politics of Confrontation*. New York: Appleton-Century-Crofts, 1971: 202.

22. Dahl, *Modern Political Analysis*, pp. 6–9.

23. Deming, *The New Economics*, pp. 106–107. Deming also added this word of caution: No number of successful examples proves a theory, but a single unexplained failure means you have to change your theory or discard it.

24. Chandler, *How to Beat Your Dad at Chess*, p. 8.

25. Martin Luther King Jr. wrote, "We are caught in an inescapable network of mutuality, tied in a single garment of destiny. Whatever affects one directly, affects all indirectly." *Letter from Birmingham Jail*, April 16, 1963.

26. Jung, *Symbols of Transformation*, p. 357.

27. Jung, *Civilization in Transition*, p. 237.

28. Rosinski, *Power and Human Destiny*, p. 202. See also Williamson and Pang (33–34) and Brieschke (53) in Longmire, *Untying the Tongue*.

29. Freud, *Civilization and Its Discontents*, pp. 33–34.

30. Camus, *The Rebel*, p. 189.

31. Schumpeter, *Capitalism*.

Chapter 4

1. Block, *Stewardship*, p. 39.

2. Lasswell, *Power and Personality*, pp. 94–95; 38–39.

3. Jung, *Psychological Types*, p. 360.

4. Jung, *Two Essays*, p. 114.

5. Robert Dahl says it is unfair to treat James Madison as a political theorist because "He was writing and speaking for his time, not for the ages." At the same time, however, Dahl acknowledges Madison's (and I would add Hamilton's and Jay's) monumental contribution to the way we continue to think about democracy and American politics. See Dahl, *A Preface to Democratic Theory*, p. 5.

6. Harold Lasswell considered Freud an "epochal figure." One example of the influence of psychoanalysis on political science is Lasswell's "triple-appeal principle," which divides behavior patterns into three categories: impulse, conscience, and reason. The purpose of this system is to improve political management by systematizing micropolitics and "person–to–person" relations. See Lasswell, *The Analysis of Political Behavior*, pp. 181–186.

7. Strausz–Hupé, *Power and Community*, p. 2.

8. Hillman, *Re–Visioning Psychology*, p. 188.

9. Ibid., pp. 244–245.

10. Jung, *Civilization in Transition*, p. 138.

11. Russell, *Authority and the Individual*, p. 5.

12. Jung, *Psychological Types*, p. 448 (italics added).

13. Spitz, *Democracy and the Challenge of Power*, pp. 7–10.

14. Beetham, *The Legitimation of Power*, pp. 234–235.

15. Kappeler, *The Will to Violence*, pp. 208–209.

16. Hobbes, *Leviathan*, Chapter X.

17. Hobbes, *Leviathan*, Chapter I, Section 12; Chapter XXI.

18. Herzog, *Happy Slaves*, p. ix.

19. Locke, *Second Treatise of Government*, Chapter 8, Section 95. See also Sections 104, 106, and 190. In James Barber's book about the process of decision–making in committees,

he concluded the ability to gain consent was an indicator of interpersonal power. See Barber, *Power in Committees*, pp. 136–137.

20. Herzog, *Happy Slaves*, p. 174.

21. Sharp, *The Politics of Nonviolent Action*, pp. 26; 30–31.

22. Jung, *Psychological Types*, p. 60.

23. Jung, *Archetypes*, p. 131.

24. Hillman, *Re–Visioning Psychology*, p. 147 (italics original).

25. Jung, *Civilization*, p. 22.

26. Jung, *Archetypes*, p. 125.

27. Iyer, *The Moral and Political Thought of Mahatma Gandhi*, p. 173.

28. Wolfgang Saxon, "Raghavan Narasimhan Iyer, 65, An Expert on East–West Cultures." *New York Times*, June 24, 1995.

29. Iyer, *Parapolitics*, pp. 96–97.

30. Ibid., p. 28.

31. Jung, *Archetypes*, pp. 40, 145, 198, 348.

32. Jung, *Development*, p. 197.

33. Iyer, *The Moral and Political Thought*, p. 133.

34. Iyer, *Parapolitics*, p. 315.

35. Allen, *The Power of Feminist Theory*, p. 19. Also from personal correspondence with the author, November 30, 2012.

36. Sampson, *The Psychology of Power*, pp. 20, 45.

37. Freud, *The Ego and the Id*, p. 3.

38. Freud, *Civilization and Its Discontents*, pp. 36–37.

39. Sampson, *The Psychology of Power*, pp. 138–139.

40. "When power is confined to the members of one sect, there is inevitably a severe ideological censorship. Sincere believers

will be anxious to spread the true faith; others will be content with outward conformity." In Russell, *Power*, p. 196. Jung remarks on the challenge of reading the field in his essay on the psychology of rebirth, in *Archetypes*, pp. 116–118.

41. Rokeach, *Beliefs*, p. 124.

42. Ibid.

43. Rokeach, *The Nature of Human Values*, pp. 7–8.

44. Friedan, *The Feminine Mystique*, p. 325. See also Maslow, *Toward a Psychology of Being*.

45. Jung, *Archetypes*, p. 60.

46. Hillman, *Kinds of Power*, p. 153.

Chapter 5

1. Edelman, *The Symbolic Uses of Politics*, pp. 5, 10, 20.

2. Adams, *Energy & Structure*, p. 108.

3. Cohen, *Two-Dimensional Man*, p. 23. Cohen's definition is close to what political scientist Robert Tucker called a *sustaining myth*, which represents a society's ideal cultural patterns, and has the power to hold a society together even though its members are dispersed or occupy no territory. See Tucker, *Politics as Leadership*, pp. 99–100; 143–144.

4. Jung, *Psychological Types*, p. 377.

5. Symbolic power is the ability to produce belief, and belief in the legitimacy of words and slogans is what makes symbolic power so potent. See Bourdieu, *Language and Symbolic Power*, p. 170.

6. Jung, *Civilization*, p. 440. Khoshkish, *The Socio–political Complex*, p. 146.

7. Psychologist David Winter retold the legend of Don Juan to explain the power motive. Why devote an entire chapter

to a mythic archetype rather than a real person? Because, he said, "the irrelevant features and distracting details have been stripped away. Like most legendary figures, Don Juan is not concerned with the trivia of daily life: he stands forth as a clear and forceful archetype." See Winter, *The Power Motive*, p. 164.

8. Schermerhorn, *Society and Power*, pp. 2–6.

9. Jung, *Archetypes*, p. 84.

10. Ascher and Hirschfelder–Ascher, *Revitalizing Political Psychology*, p. 17.

11. Jung, *Archetypes*, p. 93.

12. Ibid., p. 101. According to Karl Mannheim, "Interaction in power relations is not based on fear alone but on mutual response, which is perhaps the more general source of human control." See Mannheim, *Freedom*, p. 49.

13. Edelman, *The Symbolic Uses of Politics*, p. 5.

14. Jung, *Two Essays*, p. 192.

15. Bailey, *Morality and Expediency*, p. 127.

16. Bailey, *The Tactical Uses of Passion*, pp. 53–54.

Chapter 6

1. Lasswell, *Power and Personality*, p. 19. Robert Strausz–Hupé asked a similar question: "Is there an arch-type [sic] of power–seeking man, a man so disposed by basic character formation towards his fellowmen that all his thoughts and feelings congeal in the lust for domination?" See Strausz–Hupé, *Power and Community*, p.26.

2. This is Lasswell's maximization postulate, which is a highly complex psychological and political calculation. See Ascher and Hirschfelder-Ascher, *Revitalizing Political Psychology*, p. 11.

3. Lasswell, *Power and Personality*, p. 38.

4. Edelman, *The Symbolic Uses of Politics*, p. 75.

5. Wildavsky, *The Nursing Father*, p. 185.

6. McFarland, *Power and Leadership*, pp. 154–155 (italics original).

7. Parenti, *Power and the Powerless*, p. 10.

8. Boulding, *Three Faces of Power*, pp. 25–28, 38. See also Sites, *Control*, pp. 153–156.

9. Parenti, *Power and the Powerless*, p. 7.

10. Bailey, *Stratagems and Spoils*, p. 76.

11. Lasswell, *Power and Personality*, p. 14. Sanctioned expectation is Lasswell's alternate definition of power.

12. Hillman, *Kinds of Power*, p. 225. According to Jung, the archetypes are "the ruling powers, the gods, images of the dominant laws and principles." See Jung, *Two Essays*, p. 95.

13. *Lawrence of Arabia*. Columbia Pictures, 1962. Screenplay by Robert Bolt. Directed by David Lean.

14. Iyer, *The Moral and Political Thought of Mahatma Gandhi*, p. 143.

15. Burns, *Leadership*, p. 417.

16. Johnson, *Address Before a Joint Session of the Congress*, November 27, 1963.

17. Interview by William C. Taylor, "The Leader of the Future," *Fast Company*, June 1999.

18. Jung, *Archetypes*, p. 210.

19. Kano, *Mind Over Muscle*, pp. 130–131.

20. Iyer, *The Moral and Political Thought*, p. 139.

21. Abraham Kaplan, in Kahn and Boulding, *Power and Conflict in Organizations*, p. 28. See Friedman, "Why How Matters."

22. Wildavsky, *The Nursing Father*, p. 1.

23. Ibid., p. 122.

24. George Orwell, *Animal Farm*. New York: Harcourt, Brace and Company, 1946.

25. Kayden, *Surviving Power*, pp. 55–56.

26. Sociologist Ritchie Lowry reaches a similar conclusion in his book on small-town leadership. Effective leadership requires a common frame of reference, he says, which involves ongoing interaction, communication, and intimacy. See Lowry, *Who's Running This Town?*, pp. 160–161. See also Kreisberg, *Transforming Power*, p. 178.

27. Camus, *The Rebel*, p. 138.

28. Jung, *Psychological Types*, p. 404.

29. Jung, *Civilization*, p. 142.

30. Jung, *Archetypes*, pp. 38–39.

31. Camus, *The Rebel*, pp. 19–22.

32. Ohmae, *The Mind of the Strategist*, p. 276.

33. Senge, *The Fifth Discipline*, pp. 142, 226.

34. Kahn and Boulding, *Power and Conflict*, pp. 2–3.

35. Hillman, *The Myth of Analysis*, p. 38.

36. Masters, *Machiavelli*, pp. 105–106.

37. Gamson, *Power and Discontent*, p. 118.

38. Brislin, *The Art of Getting Things Done*, pp. 97–99.

39. *The Godfather*. Paramount Pictures, 1972. Screenplay by Mario Puzo and Francis Ford Coppola. Directed by Francis Ford Coppola.

40. *The Matrix*. Warner Brothers Pictures, 1999. Written and directed by Larry and Andy Wachowski.

41. See Ohmae, *The Mind of the Strategist.*

42. Reich, *The Work of Nations*, pp. 85, 88.

43. Greene, *48 Laws of Power*, p. 87 (italics original).

44. Machiavelli, *The Prince*, Chapter XVII.

45. Deming, *Out of the Crisis*, pp. 23–24, 59–60.

46. Iyer, *Parapolitics*, pp. 96–97.

47. J.K. Rowling, *Harry Potter and the Sorcerer's Stone.* New York: Scholastic, 1997, p. 297.

48. Hillman, *Kinds of Power*, p. 211.

49. According to David Easton, this type of response (the withdrawal type) deprives an issue of political value, which is typical for taboo subjects, wedge issues, and other issues with the potential to generate conflict or prevent agreement on other issues. See Easton, *A Systems Analysis*, pp. 262–263.

50. Foucault, *Discipline and Punish*, p. 231.

51. Ibid., pp. 237–239.

52. Derbeken, "Judo Champ."

53. Godwin, *Clintonomics*, pp. 246–247.

54. Iyer, *The Moral and Political Thought*, pp. 59–60.

55. Foucault, *Discipline and Punish*, p. 104.

56. Ibid., pp. 104–114.

57. *Reversal of Fortune.* Warner Brothers, 1990. Screenplay by Nicholas Kazan. Directed by Barbet Schroeder.

58. Iyer, *Parapolitics*, p. 28.

59. Gandhi. *Non-Violent Resistance*, p. 74.

60. Stiehm, *Nonviolent Power*, pp. 21–22.

61. Tolstoy, *The Kingdom of God.* Project Gutenberg EBook: *www.gutenberg.org*, Chapter VIII.

62. Gandhi, *NoniViolent Resistance*, p. 3.

63. Thoreau, *On the Duty of Civil Disobedience. www.gutenberg. net.*

64. Ibid.

65. Jack London, *The Call of the Wild.* 1903. Project Gutenberg Ebook: *www.gutenberg.org.*

66. "Opportunism." *Webster's New World College Dictionary*, 3rd Ed. New York: Simon and Schuster, 1996: 950.

67. I relied primarily on two translations of *the Art of War*: Thomas Cleary, *Classics of Strategy and Counsel, Volume One* (Boston: Shambala, 2000), and Lionel Giles (Project Gutenberg EBook, 1994, *www.gutenberg.org*).

68. *Patton.* 20th Century Fox, 1970. Screenplay by Francis Ford Coppola and Edmund H. North. Directed by Franklin J. Schaffner.

69. Churchill, *The Gathering Storm.*

70. Canetti, *Crowds and Power*, p. 227.

71. Ibid.

72. Ibid., pp. 284–285.

73. Frankl, *Man's Search for Meaning*, p. 2.

74. Ibid., p. 18.

75. Ibid., p. 30.

Chapter 7

1. Kelling and Wilson, "Broken Windows." See also Kelling and Coles, *Fixing Broken Windows*.

2. Marcus Aurelius, *Meditations,* Book IV, Part 3. Project Gutenberg EBook: *www.gutenberg.org*.

3. Jung, *Civilization*, p. 149.

4. Frankl, *Man's Search for Meaning*, p. 67.

5. Jung, *Civilization*, p. 286.

6. Camus, *The Rebel*, p. 208.

Appendix

1. For more information, contact the U.S. Department of Health & Human Services, Washington, D.C., 20201. *www .stopbullying.gov/index.html*.

2. For more information, contact the Workplace Bullying Institute, Bellingham, Wash., 98228. *www.workplacebullying. org*

3. Job 38:11.

4. Swomley, *Liberation Ethics*, p. 24.

5. Iyer, *The Moral and Political Thought of Mahatma Gandhi*, p. 143.

Bibliography

Adams, Richard Newbold. *Energy & Structure: A Theory of Social Power.* Austin, Texas: University of Texas Press, 1975.

Allen, Amy. *The Power of Feminist Theory: Domination, Resistance, Solidarity.* Boulder, Colo.: Westview Press, 1999.

Argyris Chris. *Personality and Organization: The Conflict Between System and the Individual.* New York: Garland, 1987.

Argyris, Chris, and Donald A. Schön. *Organization Learning: A Theory of Action Perspective.* Reading, Mass.: Addison-Wesley, 1978.

————. *Organizational Learning II: Theory, Method, and Practice.* Reading, Mass.: Addison-Wesley, 1996.

————. *Theory in Practice.* San Francisco: Jossey-Bass, 1974.

Aristotle. *Politics: A Treatise on Government.* The Project Gutenberg EBook produced by Eric Eldred. Translated from Greek by William Ellis. London and Toronto: J. M. Dent & Sons, 1928.

Ascher, William, and Barbara Hirschfelder-Ascher. *Revitalizing Political Psychology: The Legacy of Harold D. Lasswell.* Mahwah, N.J.: Lawrence Erlbaum, 2005.

Aurelius, Marcus. *Meditations.* Produced by J. Boulton. Project Gutenberg EBook. Project Gutenberg Literary Archive Foundation, 809 North 1500 West, Salt Lake City, Utah, 84116. *www.gutenberg.org.*

Bailey, F.G. *Morality and Expediency: The Folklore of Academic Politics.* Foreword by Alfred Harris. Chicago: Aldine, 1977.

————. *Stratagems and Spoils: A Social Anthropology of Politics.* New York: Schoken Books, 1969.

————. *The Tactical Uses of Passion: An Essay on Power, Reason, and Reality.* Ithaca, N.Y.: Cornell University Press, 1983.

Barber, James David. *Power in Committees: An Experiment in the Governmental Process.* Chicago: Rand McNally, 1966.

Becker, Carl. *Progress and Power.* Intro. by Leo Gershoy. New York: Alfred A. Knopf, 1949.

Beetham, David. *The Legitimation of Power.* Atlantic Highlands, N.J.: Humanities Press International, 1991.

Berle, Adolf A. *Power.* New York: Harcourt, Brace & World, 1969.

Block, Peter. *The Empowered Manager: Positive Political skills at Work.* San Francisco: Jossey-Bass, 1991.

————. *Stewardship: Choosing Service over Self-Interest.* San Francisco: Berret-Koehler, 1993.

Boulding, Kenneth. *Three Faces of Power.* Newbury Park, Calif.: Sage, 1989.

Bourdieu, Pierre. *Acts of Resistance: Against the Tyranny of the Market.* Trans. by Richard Nice. New York: The Free Press, 1998.

———. *Distinction: A Social Critique of the Judgement of Taste.* Trans. by Richard Nice. Cambridge, Mass.: Harvard University Press, 1984.

———. *Language and Symbolic Power.* Ed. and Intro by John B. Thompson. Trans. by Gino Raymond and Matthew Adamson. Cambridge, Mass.: Harvard University Press, 1994.

Branden, Nathaniel. *The Psychology of Self-Esteem: a Revolutionary Approach to Self-Understanding that Launched a New Era in Modern Psychology.* San Francisco: Jossey-Bass, 2001.

Brislin, Richard W. *The Art of Getting Things Done: A Practical Guide to the Use of Power.* New York: Praeger, 1991.

Burns, James MacGregor. *Leadership.* New York: Harper & Row, 1978.

Burton-Rose, Daniel. "The Lit Interview: Thomas Cleary." *San Francisco Bay Guardian*, Vol. 40, No. 4, October 26–November 1, 2005.

Calhoun, Craig, Edward LiPuma, and Moishe Postone. *Bourdieu: Critical Perspectives.* Chicago: University of Chicago Press, 1993.

Camus, Albert. *The Rebel.* Foreword by Herbert Read. Trans. by Anthony Bower. New York: Alfred A. Knopf, 1954.

Canetti, Elias. *Crowds and Power.* Trans. by Carol Stewart. New York: Seabury Press, 1978.

Cartwright, Dorwin, ed. *Studies in Social Power.* Ann Arbor: University of Michigan, 1959.

Chadwick, Richard. "Social Science and the Social Interest: Three Paradigms and a Synthesis." Unpublished manuscript. September, 1974.

Chancer, Lynn S. *Sadomasochism in Everyday Life: the Dynamics of Power and Powerlessness.* New Brunswick, N.J.: Rutgers University Press, 1992.

Chandler, Murray. *How to Beat Your Dad at Chess.* London: Gambit, 2010.

Churchill, Winston S. *The Gathering Storm: The Second World War, Vol. 1*. Boston: Houghton Mifflin, 1948.

Cleary, Thomas. *Classics of Strategy and Counsel*, Volumes. 1-3. Boston: Shambala, 2000.

Clegg, Stewart. *Power, Rule and Domination: A Critical and Empirical Understanding of Power in Sociological Theory and Organizational Life*. London: Routledge & Kegan Paul, 1975.

Cohen, Abner. *Two-Dimensional Man: An Essay on the Anthropology of Power and Symbolism in Complex Society*. London: Routledge & Kegan Paul, 1974.

Covey, Stephen R. *Principle-Centered Leadership*. New York: Simon & Schuster, 1992.

————. *The 7 Habits of Highly Effective People: Restoring the Character Ethic*. New York: Simon & Schuster, 1989.

Dahl, Robert A. *Democracy and Its Critics*. New Haven, Conn.: Yale University Press, 1989.

————. *Modern Political Analysis, Second Edition*. Englewood Cliffs, N.J.: Prentice Hall, 1970.

————. *A Preface to Democratic Theory*. Chicago: University of Chicago Press, 1965.

Deming, W. Edwards. *The New Economics for Industry, Government and Education*. Cambridge, Mass.: MIT, 1993.

————. *Out of the Crisis*. Cambridge, Mass.: MIT, 1986.

Derbeken, Jaxon Van. "Judo Champ Jailed in Train Station Beating." *San Francisco Chronicle*, October 2, 2009.

Dingwell, Robert. "Language, Law, and Power: Ethnomethodology, Conversation Analysis, and the Politics of Law and Society Studies." *Law & Social Inquiry*, Vol. 25, No. 3 (Summer 2000).

Duke, James T. *Conflict and Power in Social Life*. Provo, Utah: Brigham Young University Press, 1976.

Easton, David. *A Framework for Political Analysis.* Englewood Cliffs, N.J.: Prentice-Hall, 1965.

———. *A Systems Analysis of Political Life.* Chicago: University of Chicago Press, 1979.

Easton, David, ed. *Varieties of Power.* Englewood Cliffs, N.J.: Prentice-Hall, 1966.

Edelman, Murray. *The Symbolic Uses of Politics.* Urbana: University of Illinois Press, 1964.

Elgin, Suzette Haden. *The Gentle Art of Verbal Self-Defense.* Revised and Updated Edition. New York: Barnes & Noble, 2009.

Ellis, Joseph P. *Founding Brothers: The Revolutionary Generation.* New York: Vintage Books, 2000.

Endsley, Mica. "Toward a Theory of Situation Awareness in Dynamic Systems." *Human Factors* 37.1 (1995): 36.

Foucault, Michel. *Discipline and Punish: The Birth of the Prison.* Trans. by Alan Sheridan. New York: Random House, 1977.

Frankl, Viktor E. *Man's Search for Meaning: An Introduction to Logotherapy.* Preface by Gordon W. Allport. Revised edition, trans. by Ilse Lasch. New York: Clarion, 1970.

Frederick, William C. *Values, Nature, and Culture in the American Corporation.* New York: Oxford University Press, 1995.

Friedan, Betty. *The Feminine Mystique.* New York: W.W. Norton, 1963.

Friedman, Thomas L. "Why How Matters." *The New York Times*, October 15, 2008.

Freud, Sigmund. *Civilization and Its Discontents.* Trans. and ed. by James Strachey. New York: W.W. Norton, 1961.

———. *The Ego and the Id.* Trans. by Joan Riviere. Ed. by James Strachey. New York: W.W. Norton, 1962.

———. *Totem and Taboo: Some Points of Argument between the Mental Lives of Savages and Neurotics.* Trans. by James Strachey. New York: W.W. Norton, 1950.

Fromm, Erich. *To Have or To Be?* World Perspectives Series, Vol. 50., ed. by Ruth Nanda Anshen. New York: Harper & Row, 1976.

———. *The Sane Society.* New York: Holt, Rinehart and Winston, 1955.

———. "Values, Psychology, and Human Existence." Abraham H, Maslow, ed. *New Knowledge in Human Values.* Foreword by Pitirim A. Sorokin. New York: Harper & Row, 1959: 151-164.

Galbraith, John Kenneth. *Anatomy of Power.* Boston: Houghton Mifflin, 1983.

Gamson, William A. *Power and Discontent.* Homewood, Ill.: Dorsey Press, 1968.

Gandhi, M.K. *An Autobiography or The Story of My Experiments with Truth.* Trans. by Mahadev Desai. Ahmedabad: Navajivan, 1999.

———. *Non-Violent Resistance.* Ed. by Bharatan Kumarappa. New York: Schocken Books, 1972.

Gornick, Vivian, and Barbara K. Moran, eds. *Woman in Sexist Society: Studies in Power and Powerlessness.* New York: Basic Books, 1971.

Greene, Robert. *48 Laws of Power.* New York: Viking, 1998.

Greenstein, Fred I. *Personality and Politics: Problems, Evidence, Inference and Conceptualization.* New York: W.W. Norton, 1975.

———. *The Presidential Difference: Leadership Style from FDR to Barack Obama, 3rd ed.* Princeton, N.J.: Princeton University Press, 2009.

Guinote, Ana, and Theresa K. Vescio, eds. *The Social Psychology of Power.* New York: Guilford Press, 2010.

Haden Elgin, Suzette. *The Gentle Art of Verbal Self-Defense.* (Revised and Updated.) New York: Fall River Press, 2009.

Hendel, Samuel, ed. *The Politics of Confrontation.* New York: Appleton-Century-Crofts, 1971.

Herzog, Don. *Happy Slaves: A Critique of Consent Theory.* Chicago: University of Chicago Press, 1989.

Hesse, Hermann. *Siddhartha*. Trans. by Hilda Rosner. New York: New Directions, 1951.

Hillman, James. *Kinds of Power: A Guide to its Intelligent Uses*. New York: Currency Doubleday, 1995.

———. *The Myth of Analysis: Three Essays in Archetypal Psychology*. Evanston, Ill.: Northwestern University Press, 1972.

———. *Re-Visioning Psychology*. New York: Harper & Row, 1975.

Hobbes, Thomas. *Leviathan*. Project Gutenberg EBook, *www.gutenberg. org*.

Hunter, Floyd. *Community Power Structure: A Study of Decision Makers*. Chapel Hill: University of North Carolina Press, 1953.

Iyer, Raghavan N. *The Moral and Political Thought of Mahatma Gandhi*, 2nd ed. London: Concord Grove Press, 1983.

———. *Parapolitics: Toward the City of Man*. New York: Oxford University Press, 1979.

Janeway, Elizabeth. *Powers of the Weak*. New York: Alfred A. Knopf, 1980.

Janowitz, Morris, ed. *Community Political Systems*. Glencoe, Ill.: The Free Press, 1961.

Jung, Carl G. *The Archetypes and the Collective Unconscious* (Collected Works, Vol. 9, Part 1) Ed. by Herbert Read. Trans. by R.F.C. Hull. Princeton, N.J.: Princeton University Press, 1969.

———. *Civilization in Transition* (Collected Works, Vol. 10) Ed. by Herbert Read. Trans. by R.F.C. Hull. Princeton, N.J.: Princeton University Press, 1970.

———. *The Development of Personality* (Collected Works, Vol. 17) Ed. by Herbert Read. Trans. by R.F.C. Hull. Princeton, N.J.: Princeton University Press, 1954.

———. *Freud and Psychoanalysis* (Collected Works, Vol. 4) Ed. by Herbert Read. Trans. by R.F.C. Hull. Princeton, N.J.: Princeton University Press, 1961.

————. *Psychological Types* (Collected Works, Vol. 6) Ed. by Herbert Read. Trans. by H.G. Baynes. Revised by R.F.C. Hull. Princeton, N.J.: Princeton University Press, 1971.

————. *Symbols of Transformation* (Collected Works, Vol. 5) Ed. by Herbert Read. Trans. by R.F.C. Hull. Princeton, N.J.: Princeton University Press, 1967.

————. *Two Essays on Analytical Psychology* (Collected Works, Vol. 7) Ed. by Herbert Read. Trans. by R.F.C. Hull. Princeton, N.J.: Princeton University Press, 1966.

Kahn, Robert L. and Elise Boulding, eds. *Power and Conflict in Organizations.* New York: Basic Books, 1964.

Kano, Jigoro. *Mind Over Muscle: Writings from the Founder of Judo.* Foreword by Yukimitsu Kano. Ed. by Naoki Murata. Trans. by Nancy H. Ross. Tokyo: Kodansha, 2005.

Kappeler, Susanne. *The Will to Violence: The Politics of Personal Behavior.* New York: Teachers College Press, 1995.

Kayden, Xandra. *Surviving Power: The Experience of Power—Exercising It and Giving It Up.* New York: The Free Press, 1990.

Kelling, George L., and Catherine M. Coles. *Fixing Broken Windows: Restoring Order and Reducing Crime in Our Communities.* New York: The Free Press, 1996.

Kelling, George L., and James Q. Wilson. "Broken Windows." *The Atlantic*, March 1982.

Khoshkish, A. *The Socio-political Complex: An Interdisciplinary Approach to Political Life.* New York: Pergamon Press, 1979.

King, Stephen. *On Writing: A Memoir of the Craft.* New York: Scribner, 2010.

Kornhauser, Arthur, ed. *Problems of Power in American Democracy.* Detroit: Wayne State University Press, 1957.

Kreisberg, Seth. *Transforming Power: Domination, Empowerment, and Education.* Albany, N.Y.: SUNY Press, 1992.

Lasswell, Harold D. *The Analysis of Political Behavior: An Empirical Approach*. Hamden, Conn.: Archon Books, 1966.

———. *Power and Personality*. New York: W.W. Norton, 1976.

———. *Who Gets What, When, How*. Cleveland, Ohio: World Publishing Company, 1968.

———. *World Politics and Personal Insecurity*. New York: The Free Press, 1965.

Lenski, Gerhard A. *Power and Privilege: A Theory of Social Stratification*. Chapel Hill: University of North Carolina Press, 1984.

Liebert, Roland J., and Allen W. Imershein, eds. *Power, Paradigms, and Community Research*. London: Sage Publications, 1977.

Lipsey, R.G., and Kelvin Lancaster. "The General Theory of Second Best." *Review of Economic Studies* 24: 11–32.

Locke, John. *Second Treatise of Government*. The Project Gutenberg EBook. *www.gutenberg.org/catalog/world/readfile?fk_files=3275825*.

Loewenstein, Karl. *Political Power and the Governmental Process*. Chicago: University of Chicago Press, 1957.

Longmire, Linda, and Lisa Merrill, eds. *Untying the Tongue: Gender, Power, and the Word*. Westport, Conn.: Greenwood Press, 1998.

Lowry, Ritchie P. *Who's Running This Town? Community Leadership and Social Change*. New York: Harper Torchbooks, 1968.

Machiavelli, Nicolo. The Prince. Project Gutenberg EBook. *www.gutenberg.org*

MacIver, Robert. *On Community, Society, and Power*. Ed. by Leon Bramson. Chicago: University of Chicago Press, 1970.

Mann, Michael. *The Sources of Power, Volume I*. Cambridge, Mass.: Cambridge University Press, 1986.

Mannheim, Karl. *Freedom, Power, and Democratic Planning*. New York: Oxford University Press, 1950.

Maslow, Abraham H. *Toward a Psychology of Being*. New York: D. Van Nostrand Company, 1968.

Maslow, Abraham H., ed. *New Knowledge in Human Values*. Foreword by Pitirim A. Sorokin. New York: Harper & Row, 1959.

Masters, Roger D. *Machiavelli, Leonardo and the Science of Power*. Notre Dame, Ind.: University of Notre Dame Press, 1996.

McFarland, Andrew S. *Power and Leadership in Pluralistic Systems*. Stanford, Calif.: Stanford University Press, 1969.

Mills, C. Wright. *The Power Elite*. 2nd ed., with a new afterword by Alan Wolfe. Oxford: Oxford University Press, 2000.

————. *Power, Politics and People: The Collected Essays of C. Wright Mills*. Ed. and Intro. by Louis Horowitz. New York: Oxford University Press, 1963.

Morgenthau, Hans J. *Politics Among Nations: The Struggle for Power and Peace*. Sixth Edition. Revised by Kenneth W. Thompson. New York: Alfred A. Knopf, 1985.

Mumby, Dennis K. *Communication and Power in Organizations: Discourse, Ideology, and Domination*. Norwood, N.J.: Ablex, 1988.

O'Neill, Thomas P., Jr., with William Novak. *Man of the House: The Life and Political Memoirs of Speaker Tip O'Neill*. New York: Random House, 1987.

Ohmae, Kenichi. *The Mind of the Strategist: The Art of Japanese Business*. New York: McGraw-Hill, 1982.

Orwell, George. *Animal Farm*. New York: Harcourt, Brace and Co., 1946.

Parenti, Michael. *Power and the Powerless*. New York: St. Martin's Press, 1978.

Peace Corps. *Culture Matters: The Peace Corps Cross-Cultural Workbook*. Washington, D.C.: U.S. Government Printing Office, 1999.

Plato. *Apology or the Death of Socrates*. Trans. by Benjamin Jowett. Project Gutenberg EBook. *www.gutenberg.org*.

———. *The Republic*. Trans. by Benjamin Jowett. Project Gutenberg EBook. *www.gutenberg.org*.

Reich, Robert B. *The Work of Nations: Preparing Ourselves for 21st Century Capitalism*. New York: Alfred A. Knopf, 1991.

Rokeach, Milton. *Beliefs, Attitudes, and Values: A Theory of Organization and Change*. San Francisco: Jossey-Bass, 1968.

———. *The Nature of Human Values*. New York: Free Press, 1973.

Rubinoff, Lionel. *The Pornography of Power*. Chicago: Quadrangle Books, 1968.

Rosinski, Herbert. *Power and Human Destiny*. Ed. by Richard P. Stebbins. Foreword by August Hecksher. New York: Praeger, 1965.

Russell, Bertrand. *Authority and the Individual*. New York: Simon and Schuster, 1949.

———. *Power: A New Social Analysis*. London: George Allen & Unwin, 1957.

Sampson, Ronald V. *The Psychology of Power*. New York: Pantheon Books, 1965.

———. *Tolstoy: The Discovery of Peace*. London: Heinemann, 1973.

Schermerhorn, Richard A. *Society and Power*. Foreword by Charles H. Page. New York: Random House, 1961.

Schumpeter, Joseph A. *Capitalism, Socialism and Democracy*. New York: Harper and Row, 1976.

Senge, Peter M. *The Fifth Discipline: The Art and Practice of the Learning Organization*. New York: Currency/Doubleday, 1990.

Sharp, Gene. *The Politics of Nonviolent Action*. Boston: Porter Sargent, 1973.

Sites, Paul. *Control: The Basis of Social Order*. New York: Dunellen, 1973.

Spitz, David. *Democracy and the Challenge of Power*. New York: Columbia University Press, 1958.

Stiehm, Judith. *Nonviolent Power: Active and Passive Resistance in America.* Lexington, Mass.: DC Heath & Co., 1972.

Strausz-Hupé, Robert. *Power and Community.* New York: Frederick A. Praeger, 1956.

Swingle, Paul G. *The Management of Power.* New York: John Wiley & Sons, 1976.

Tolstoy, Leo. *The Kingdom of God is Within You: Christianity not as a Mystic Religion but as a New Theory of Life.* Trans. by Constance Garnett. Project Gutenberg EBook. *www.gutenberg.org.*

Tucker, Robert C. *Politics as Leadership.* Columbia: University of Missouri Press, 1981.

Tzu, Sun. *The Art of War.* Edited and with a Foreword by James Clavell. New York: Dell, 1983. (There are numerous other translations of this book.)

Vlastos, Stephen, ed. *Mirror of Modernity: Invented Traditions of Japan.* Berkeley: University of California Press, 1998.

Von Clausewitz, Carl. *On War.* Trans. by J.J. Graham (1874). Intro. by F.N. Maude. Project Gutenberg EBook. *www.gutenberg.org.*

Von Bertalanffy, Ludwig. *General System Theory, Foundations, Development, Applications.* New York: George Braziller, 1968.

Wartenberg, Thomas E. *The Forms of Power: From Domination to Transformation.* Philadelphia: Temple University Press, 1990.

Watts, Richard J. *Power in Family Discourse.* New York: Mouton de Gruyter, 1991.

Weber, Max. *The Theory of Social and Economic Organization.* Talcott Parsons, ed. Glencoe, Ill.: The Free Press, 1957.

Westwood, Sallie. *Power and the Social.* New York: Routledge, 2002.

Wildavsky, Aaron. *The Nursing Father: Moses as a Political Leader.* Tuscaloosa: University of Alabama Press, 1984.

Winter, David G. *The Power Motive.* New York: The Free Press, 1973.

Index

About the Author

Jack Godwin, PhD, is a political scientist whose appeal spans the political spectrum. His previous book was *Clintonomics*, which former Defense Secretary Leon Panetta called "a must-read." Christopher Ruddy, the conservative publisher of Newsmax.com, said, "I couldn't agree more with Panetta's assessment." Jack began his career as a Peace Corps volunteer in Gabon, West Africa. He has a doctorate from the University of Hawaii, and degrees from San Francisco State University and the University of California, Berkeley. He is a four-time Fulbright scholar and a member of the Pacific Council on International Policy. In *The Office Politics Handbook*, he draws from his personal experience in business and government, and his repertoire of anecdotes and archetypes from history, literature, and film to entertain and educate readers about interpersonal relationships, politics, and leadership.